Basic Accounting Practice
Teacher's Guide

MWE Glautier · B Underdown · AC Clark

Third edition

Pitman

PITMAN PUBLISHING
128 Long Acre, London WC2E 9AN

© Guardjust Ltd, B Underdown and A C Clark 1979, 1980, 1985

First published in Great Britain 1979
Second edition 1980, reprinted 1983 twice, 1984
Third edition 1985
Reprinted 1986, 1987 twice, 1988

British Library Cataloguing in Publication Data
Glautier, M.W.E.
  Basic accounting practice.—3rd ed.
  Teachers' guide
  1. Accounting
  I. Title   II. Underdown, B   III. Clark, A.C.
  657   HF5635

  ISBN 0-273-02427-2

Printed and bound in Great Britain
by George Over Limited, London and Rugby

Basic Accounting Practice
Teacher's Guide

Contents

Preface

The purpose of this Guide is to provide a set of suggested answers to the problems posed in *Basic Accounting Practice*. Accordingly, the structure of the material reflects the order found in the text, i.e.

Part 1   Financial Accounting

Part 2   Accounting for Planning and Control

Part 3   Case Problems and Analysis

It will be appreciated that with a number of the suggested answers teachers may find themselves favouring a different viewpoint. It is not our intention to provide a monolithic type of treatment to our subject matter. Rather we hope that the suggested answers will provide a basis for discussion as well as instruction. This is particularly true in the treatment of the case problems found in Part 3. Our purpose in posing a series of progressively more difficult questions on each case was to provide teachers and students with an expanding view of the accounting problems involved and the complexities which arise when these problems are considered. In each case these problems should not be regarded as exhaustive, and for this reason we have been careful in this text to provide guidelines to the treatment of the case problems which are intended to serve only as indicating a likely entry into discussion. We hope that teachers will encourage rather than restrict the discussion of these case problems using our guidelines as stepping stones.

We have indicated where it may be found convenient to treat some of the questions found in *Basic Accounting Practice* in sections rather than as an entire question to be dealt with at one and the same time. This is because some of these questions contain accounting elements of possible difficulty.

Throughout this text our intention has been to provide a range of material appropriate to first-year courses in accounting. This approach reflects a standpoint adopted in the *Accounting Theory and Practice* series. On occasions it will be found useful to refer to *Accounting Theory and Practice* for an expanded discussion of ideas that may be dealt with more perfunctorily in *Basic Accounting Practice*. We hope that teachers will appreciate the variety of material, the range of problems found in the questions and, hopefully, will communicate to us their views on the appropriateness of our suggested answers to the teaching situations.

M.W.E.G./B.U./A.C.C.

Part 1 Financial Accounting
Chapter 1

QUESTION 1

(a) £ 2,200 Capital
(b) £14,856 Assets
(c) £ 7,978 Liabilities

QUESTION 2

	1	2	3	4	Change in Totals of Accounting Equation	
a			✓		Net increase	£ 5,000
b			✓		Net increase	£ 2,600
c	✓				No change	
d			✓		Net increase	£12,000
e				✓	Net decrease	£ 1,000
f				✓	Net decrease	£ 175
g		✓			No change	
h				✓	Net decrease	£ 120
ı	✓				No change	
j	✓				No change	
k			✓		Net increase	£ 392
l			✓		Net increase	£ 2,300

Assuming claim anticipated in prior entries.

Refrigerator account

	£
Bank	700

Rent account

	£
Bank	100

Motor van account

	£
Bank	2,000

Motor expenses account

	£			£
Bal. b/d	95	Bal. c/d		103
(3) Cash	8			
	103			103
Bal. b/d	103			

Sales account

	£			£
Bal. c/d	1,491	Cash		643
		(2) "		210
		(5) "		192
		(8) "		172
		(11) "		274
	1,491			1,491
		Bal.b.d		1,491

Purchases account

	£			£
J. Eulie	800	Bal. c/d		2,170
(1) Bank	185			
(4) Cash	150			
(6) "	195			
(10) "	200			
(12) Hermos	640			
	2,170			2,170
Bal. b/d	2,170			

J. Eulie account

	£			£
(7) Bank	800	Purchases		800

Cash account

	£			£
Bal. b/d	40	(3) Petrol		8
(2) Sales	210	(4) Pur- chases		150
(5) "	192	(6) "		195
(8) "	172	(9) Clean- ing		3
(11) "	274	(10) Pur- chases		200
		Bal. c/d		332
	888			888
Bal. b/d	332			

Cleaning account

	£			£
Cash	3	Bal. c/d		6
"	3			
	6			6
Bal. c/d	6			

Bank account

	£			£
Bal. b/d	2,505	(1)	Purchases	185
		(7)	J. Eulie	800
		(13)	Electricity	14
		(14)	Salary	25
			Bal. c/d	1,481
	2,505			2,505
Bal. c/d	1,481			

Capital account

	£			£
		Bank		6,000

Fittings account

	£			£
Bank	1,200			

Hermos Ltd account

	£
(12) Purchases	640

Electricity account

		£
(13) Bank		14

Salary account

		£
(14) Bank		25

S.A. Nary Trial Balance as at 10 July

	Debit £	Credit £
Bank account	1,481	
Capital S.A. Nary		6,000
Fittings	1,200	
Refrigerator	700	
Rent	100	
Motor van	2,000	
Motor expenses	103	
Sales		1,491
Purchases	2,170	
Cash	332	
Cleaning	6	
Hermos Ltd		640
Electricity	14	
Salary	25	
	8,131	8,131

Although this exercise is simple, the process of bringing down balances on individual accounts can be demonstrated as well as the recording system. Additionally, we have found that some students beginning a course of accounting do experience confusion regarding the function of the trial balance and its preparation. The fact that it is merely a summarized copy of existing accounts can be stressed at this point.

QUESTION 4

(a)

Bank account

	£		£
(1) Bal.b/d	5,321	(4) Wages	142
(12) Cash	250	(10) Repairs	27
		(12) Saving equipment	2,000
		(16) Wages	158
		Bal. c/d	3,244
	5,571		5,571
Bal. b/d	3,244		

Capital account

		£
	(1) Bal.	10,113

Assets account

		£
	(1) Bal. b/d	4,792

Sales account

	£		£
Bal. c/d	931	(2) Green	65
		(5) Cash	74
		(7) Ace Hotels	350
		(9) Cash	214
		(11) "	118
		(14) SBS Ltd	110
	931		931
		Bal. b/d	931

J. Green account

	£		£
(2) Goods	65	(8) Cash	25
		Bal.b/d	40
	65		65
Bal. b.d	40		

Wages account

	£		£
(4) Bank	142	Bal. c/d	300
(16) Bank	158		
	300		300
Bal. b.d	300		

Timber Supply Co. Ltd

	£		£
(6) Returns	38	(3) Goods	974
Bal. c/d	936		
	974		974
		Bal. b/d	936

Purchases account

	£		£
(3) Goods	974	(6) Returns	38
		Bal. c/d	936
	974		974
Bal. b/d	936		

Cash account

	£		£
(5) Sales	74	(12) Bank	250
(8) Green	25	(15) Delivery	14
(9) Sales	214	Bal. c/d	167
(11) Sales	118		
	431		431
Bal. b/d	167		

Sawing equipment

	£
(13) Bank	2,000

Repairs account

	£
(10) Bank	27

Delivery account

	£
(15) Cash	14

Ace Hotels Ltd

	£
(7) Goods	350

SBS Ltd

	£
(14) Goods	110

(b) Trial Balance of Sam Barker

	Ledger (£)	Debit £	Credit £
Bank account	Cash book	3,244	
Capital	General		10,113
Assets	"	4,792	
Sales account	"		931
J. Green	Debtors	40	
Wages	Expenses etc.	300	
Timber Supply Co. Ltd	Creditors		936
Purchases	Purchases etc.	936	
Cash account	Cash book	167	
Delivery expenses	Expenses etc.	14	
Ace Hotels Ltd	Debtors	350	
Repairs account	Expenses etc.	27	
Sawing equipment	General	2,000	
SBS (Decorators) Ltd	Debtors	110	
		11,980	11,980

(c) £10,113
(d) £ 936
(e) £ 500

QUESTION 5

	Debit £	Credit £
Trade creditors		13,642
Trade debtors	23,724	
Wages	14,625	
Rent and rates	6,520	
Bank balance	1,590	
Cash in hand	78	
Sales		87,428
Purchases	34,697	
Motor vehicles	18,620	
Plant and machinery	15,000	
Postage and printing	1,720	
Advertising	3,450	
Insurances	210	
Motor expenses	1,836	
Loan from bank		5,000
Capital		16,000
	122,070	122,070

Chapter 2

QUESTION 1

	A	B	C	D	E
	£	£	£	£	£
Sales	47,500	14,000	87,342	28,987	143,564
Opening stock	7,430	620	12,927	3,690	27,629
Purchases	30,100	8,490	77,100	21,347	82,231
Goods available for sale	37,530	9,110	90,027	25,037	109,860
Closing stock	8,910	710	14,250	2,190	24,300
Cost of sales	28,620	8,400	75,777	22,847	85,560
Gross profit	18,880	5,600	11,565	6,140	58,004
	47,500	14,000	87,342	28,987	143,564

QUESTION 2

	Trial Balance		Profit and loss account		Balance sheet	
	£	£	£	£	£	£
Purchases	78,326		78,326			
Sales		105,290		105,290		
Opening stock	8,425		8,425			
Closing stock		9,743		9,743		
Gross profit			28,282			
			115,033	115,033		
				28,282		
Gross profit						
Employee's salaries	12,640		12,640			
Insurance	118		118			
Rent and rates	3,750		3,750			
Repairs	874		874			
Hire of freezers	1,050		1,050			
Postages	362		362			
Printing and advertising	1,822		1,822			
Bank charges	86		86			
Motor expanses	1,736		1,736			
Telephone	210		210			
Electricity	864		864			
Net profit			4,770			
			28,282	28,282		
Capital		13,668	Net profit	4,770		18,438
Creditors		5,624				5,624
Delivery van	3,500				3,500	
Shop fittings	4,000				4,000	
Debtors	2,896				2,896	
Cash at bank	3,737				3,737	
Cash in hand	186				186	
Closing stock	9,743				9,743	
	134,325	134,325			24,062	24,062

Closing stock has been
brought into the trial
balance on both sides.

9

John Marley   Profit and loss account for the year ended 30 September 19X5

	£	£
Sales		105,290
Cost of sales		
Opening stock	8,425	
Purchases	78,326	
	86,751	
Closing stock	9,743	77,008
Gross profit		28,282
Less: Salaries	12,640	
Insurances	118	
Rent and rates	3,750	
Repairs	874	
Hire of freezers	1,050	
Postages	362	
Printing and advertising	1,822	
Bank charges	86	
Motor expenses	1,736	
Telephone	210	
Electricity	864	23,512
Net profit transferred to		4,770
Capital account		

John Marley   Balance Sheet as at 30 September 19X5

	£
Capital as at 1 October 19X4	13,668
Net profit for year ended 30 September 19X5	4,770
	18,438
Creditors	5,624
	24,062
Represented by:	
Delivery van	3,500
Shop fittings	4,000
Stock	9,743
Debtors	2,896
Cash at bank	3,737
Cash in hand	186
	24,062

QUESTION 3

The approach to answering this problem is to determine the capital at each of the two dates. Balances are listed as assets or liabilities (Dr or Cr).

Assets	1 December 19X1	30 November 19X2
	£	£
Cash in hand	24	36
Cash at bank	3,427	5,622
Tractor	5,000	3,500
Land Rover	2,100	1,600
Farm implements	3,620	4,291
Dairy equipment	7,200	6,000
Livestock	3,600	6,700
Milk Marketing Board	842	720
Seeds and growing crops	2,100	4,850
Subsidies due from Government	1,450	1,725
	29,363	35,044

Less: due to creditors

Feed and corn	1,897		2,624	
Motor expenses	84		320	
Bank loan	5,000	6,981	4,000	6,944
Difference = Capital		22,382		28,100

	£
Durant's profit is calculated:	
Capital at 30 November 19X2	28,100
Less Capital at 1 December 19X1	22,382
	5,718

To which is added the cash with-
drawn (The final bank or cash
figure at 30 November 19X2 would
have been that much greater)

52 × £25	1,300
Net profit	7,018

Note: Some students may bring the proceeds from the sale of eggs into the profit calculation. However, it can be pointed out that to do so implies that the wife's income is that of her husband.

QUESTION 4

In this problem the student is called upon to set out the data in such a way as to reveal the capital in the accounting equation.

The value of books required for the initial stock is	£6,900
Cost of shelving is	900
Cash balance required is	2,000
	9,800
Less amount from father	500
	9,300

Assuming that the credit terms granted by the various publishers are for one month and that sales occur evenly over the two months referred to in the questions then the amount required for capital will be

$$£9,300 \text{ less one half of } £6,900 =$$
$$£9,300 - £3,450 = £5,850$$

If credit terms are for two months then only

$$£9,300 - £6,900 = £2,400$$

will be required for capital.

Any assumption regarding credit terms can be accepted provided that they are correctly interpreted in the capital required calculation.

QUESTION 5

Bidston Boutique 30 June 19X6

	Trial Balance		Profit and loss account		Balance Sheet	
	Dr £	Cr £	Dr £	Cr £	Dr £	Cr £
Sales		54,365		54,365		
Purchases	35,319		35,319			
Opening stock	3,620		3,620			
Closing stock	4,390	4,390		4,390	4,390	
Gross profit			19,816			
			58,755	58,755		
				19,816		
Gross profit						
Assistants' salaries	9,200		9,200			
Rates	785		785			
Lighting and heating	674		674			
Insurance	89		89			
Sundries and postages	146		146			
Telephone	103		103			
Net profit			8,819			8,819
			19,816	19,816		
Capital		8,566				8,566
Sundry creditors						
Weldon Wholesale Clothing Ltd		840				
Monty's Model Gowns		190				
Roscoe Denim Garments Ltd		1,243				2,273
Loan - S. Owen		5,000				5,000
Freehold premises	15,500				15,500	
Fittings and display equipment	2,100				2,100	
Cash in hand	48				48	
Cash at bank	2,620				2,620	
	74,594	74,594			24,658	24,658

QUESTION 5

Bidston Boutique

Profit and loss account for the year ended 30 June 19X6

	£	£
Sales		54,365
Less Cost of sales:		
Opening stock	3,620	
Purchases	35,319	
	38,939	
Less Closing stock	4,390	34,549
Gross profit		19,816
Less: Assistants' salaries	9,200	
Rates	785	
Lighting and heating	674	
Insurance	89	
Sundries and postage	146	
Telephone	103	10,997
Net profit carried to Capital account		8,819

Balance Sheet as at 30 June 19X6

	£
Capital as at 1 July 19X5	8,566
Add Net profit for the year ended 30 June 19X6	8,819
	17,385
Loan - S. Owen	5,000
Sundry creditors	2,273
	24,658
Represented by:	
Freehold premises	15,500
Fittings and display equipment	2,100
Stock	4,390
Cash at bank	2,620
Cash in hand	48
	24,658

Chapter 3

QUESTION 1

Complete the accounts shown below by calculating the missing numbers.

Accounts	Electricity		Telephone		Wages		Rates		Motor expenses		Insurances	
	Dr £	Cr £	Dr £	Cr £	Dr £	Cr £	Dr £	Cr £	Dr £	Cr £	Dr £	Cr £
Accrual/ Prepayment b/d		120		31		1,242	900			195	350	
Cash	800		654		8,825		2,700		799		960	
Profit and loss account		750		670		8,963		3,000		1,015		890
Accrual/ Prepayment c/d	70		47		1,380			600	431			420
	870	870	701	701	10,205	10,205	3,600	3,600	1,210	1,210	1,310	1,310
Bal b/d		70		47		1,380	600			431	420	

QUESTION 2

Accounts as at 30 June 19X3 before adjustments

Bank account

	£		£
C. Aspin	2,100	Timber	3,670
Reed & Co.	1,650	Motor Exes	930
Studio Holiday Homes	4,620	Replacement of Tools	65
Casual job	1,246	Casual Labour	750
Melvin Estate	2,400	Drawings	1,560
		Bal. c/d	5,041
	12,016		12,016
Bal. b/d	5,041		

C. Aspin Capital account

	£		£
Drawings	1,560	Bank	2,100
Bal. c/d	3,575	Van	2,800
		Tools	235
	5,135		5,135
		Bal. b/d	3,575

Casual Labour account

			£
		Bank	750

Van account

	£		
C. Aspin	2,800		

Tools account

	£		
C. Aspin	235		

Purchases - materials

	£		
Bank	3,670		

Motor expenses account

	£		
Bank	930		

Replacement of Tools account

	£		
Bank	65		

Received for work done

	£		£
Bal. c/d	9,916	Reed & Co.	1,650
		Studio holiday Homes	4,620
		Casual	1,246
		Melvin Estate	2,400
	9,916		9,916
		Bal. b/d	9,916

QUESTION 2

C. Aspin. Trial Balance as at 30 June 19X3

	Dr £	Cr £
Bank account	5,041	
Capital account		3,575
Van account	2,800	
Tools account	235	
Purchases of materials	3,670	
Motor expenses	930	
Received from work done		9,916
Replacement of tools	65	
Casual labour	750	
	13,491	13,491

Profit and loss account for year ended 30 June 19X3

	£	£
Gross Earnings (9916 + 1750 - 1500)		10,166
Less: Materials (3670 - 1643)	2,027	
Casual labour	750	
Replacement of tools	65	
Motor expenses (930 + 46)	976	3,818
Net profit carried to Capital account		6,348

Balance sheet as at 30 June 19X3

		£
Capital introduced 1 July 19X2		5,135
Add net profit for year ended 30 June 19X3		6,348
		11,483
Less cash withdrawals for year		1,560
		9,923
Creditor for - Motor expenses	46	
Disputed work	1,500	1,546
		11,469

Represented by:

	£
Van	2,800
Tools	235
Stock of materials	1,643
Debtors - Studio Holiday Homes	1,750
Bank	5,041
	11,469

Notes to Required 1 & 2

(i) Aspin's cash drawings have been entered as

Dr Capital account
Cr Bank account
} with 52 × £30 = £1,560

(ii) Gross earnings are arrived at as follows (date details omitted)

	£		£
Amount in dispute carried down as Creditor	1,500	Balances earned as at 30 June 19X3	9,916
Transferred to profit and loss account as Gross Earnings	10,166	Amount taken as earned on contract with Studio Holiday Homes Ltd - now a debtor in the books	1,750
	11,666		11,666
Balance - Debtor	1,750	Balance - Creditor	1,500

(Both these balances are shown on the balance sheet)

(iii) The materials (timber) account is adjusted to record the amount of timber on hand at cost and thus shows the correct amount used during the period and also the value of closing stock. Thus the account is as follows: (date details omitted)

Purchase of Materials account

	£		£
Bank	3,670	Stock as at 30 June 19X3 c/d	1,643
		Transfer to Profit and loss account	2,027
	3,670		3,670
Balance - representing closing stock	1,643		

(iv)

Motor expenses account

	£		£
Bank	930	Transfer to profit and loss account	976
Amount due c/d	46		
	976		976
		Amount due b/d	46

The amount due £46 is shown as a creditor on the balance sheet.

(a) The gross earnings figure could be represented to the bank as £9,916 plus £1,750 = £11,666 on the grounds that the claim for £1,500 is disputed and by no means certain. The reported net profit would be £1,500 higher at £7,848.

(b) The gross earnings figure could be represented with the income tax return as £9,916 - £1,500 = £8,416 using the argument that the disputed £1,500 cannot be included until the matter is resolved and that the contract with Studio Holiday Homes Ltd is not paid for until completion and is hence not certain. The net profit would be £4,598 if this were done.

(It is not suggested that these adjustments reflect the accepted requirements for banking or taxation purposes but are offered in the hope that students can become accustomed to the lack of certainty or objectivity attached to the idea of profit.)

QUESTION 3
(All dates July. Folio references omitted)

Bank account

	£			£
1 Capital	8,000	1	Fittings	1,500
11 Hamilton Constr. Co. Ltd	200	3	Rent	75
		6	Purchases	270
		10	DK Ltd.	500
		23	Fuel	23
			Bal. c/d	5,832
	8,200			8,200
Bal b/d	5,832			

M. Plant Capital account

	£			£
		1	Bank	8,000

Fittings account

	£		£
1 Bank	1,500		

Purchases account

	£		£
2 Goods	2,400	Bal. c/d	2,698
6 Bank	270		
29 Goods	28		
	2,698		2,698
Bal. b/d	2,698		

DK Ltd account

	£			£
10 Bank	500	2	Goods	2,400
Bal. c/d	1,900			
	2,400			2,400
			Bal. b/d	1,900

Rent account

	£		£
3 Bank	75		

Cash account

	£			£
4 Sales	85	6 Wages		22
6 Sales	84	9 Postage		3
13 Sales	242	13 Wages		22
20 Sales	384	20 Wages		22
27 Sales	170	24 Cleaning		12
31 Sales	142	27 Wages		22
		30 Deliveries		8
		Bal. c/d		996
	1,107			1,107
Bal. b/d	996			

Sales account

	£		£
Bal. c/d	1,787	4 Cash	85
		5 Debtors	350
		6 Cash	84
		13 Cash	242
		20 Cash	384
		23 Debtors	330
		27 Cash	170
		31 Cash	142
	1,787		1,787
		Bal. b/d	1,787

Hamilton Construction Co.

	£		£
11 Bank	200	Goods	350
Bal. c/d	150		
	350		
		Bal. b/d	150

Wages account

	£		£
6 Cash	22	Bal. c/d	88
13 Cash	22		
20 Cash	22		
27 Cash	22		
	88		88
Bal. b/d	88		

Delivery Expenses account

	£
Cash	8

BW Ltd account

	£
29 Goods	28

Light and Heat account

	£
23 Bank	23

Postages & Sundries account

	£		£
9 Cash	3	Bal. c/d	15
24 Cleaning	12		
	15		15
Bal. b/d	15		

Midborough Education C

	£
23 Goods	330

	Trial Balance		Adjustments		Profit and loss account		Balance Sheet	
	Dr £	Cr £	Dr £	Cr £	Dr £	Cr £	Dr £	Cr £
Sales		1,787				1,787		
Purchases	2,698				2,698			
Stock	1,210		1,210	1,210		1,210	1,210	
Gross profit					299			
					2,997	2,997		
Gross profit						299		
Wages	88				88			
Light and heat	23		25		48			
Postage and sundries	15				15			
Rent	75			50	25			
Delivery expenses	8				8			
Net profit					115			115
					299	299		
Sundry Creditors								
DK Ltd		1,900						
BW Ltd		28						
Electricity				25				1,953
Sundry Debtors								
Hamilton Constr.	150							
Midboro' Edn. C	330							
Rent			50				530	
Shop fittings	1,500						1,500	
M. Plant – Capital		8,000						8,000
Bank	5,832						5,832	
Cash	996						996	
	11,715	11,715					10,068	10,068

M. Plant. Profit and loss account for month of July 19X4

	£	£
Sales		1,787
Less Cost of sales		
Purchases	2,698	
Less Closing stock	1,210	1,488
		299
Gross profit		
Less Wages	88	
Light and heat	48	
Postage and sundries	15	
Rent	25	
Delivery expenses	8	184
Net profit carried to Capital account		115

Balance Sheet as at 31 July 19X4

	£
Capital introduced	8,000
Add net profit for month of July 19X4	115
	8,115
Sundry creditors	1,953
	10,068

Represented by:	
Shop fittings	1,500
Stock	1,210
Debtors and prepayments	530
Bank	5,832
Cash	996
	10,068

QUESTION 4
(All dates are October. Folio references omitted)

Bank account

		£			£
1	Capital	11,000	1	Purchases	510
16	S. Small	1,800	7	Rent	200
22	Archer	660	9	Salaries	310
27	Smart	420	15	Van	2,300
28	Atkins	1,000	21	Dobson	735
			21	Bridges	1,422
			26	Electricity	80
				Bal. c/d	9,523
		15,080			15,080
Bal b/d		9,523			

Capital account

		£
	1 Bank	11,000

Purchases account

		£			£
1	Bank	510	15	Dobson	210
2	Dobson	945		Bal. c/d	3,882
2	Bridges	1,422			
2	Gates	365			
2	Ryan	850			
		4,092			4,092
Bal. b.d		3,882			

Boxed Ltd

		£
	3 Goods	510

Sales account

		£			£
16	Archer	40	6	Murgatroyd	212
16	Atkins	110		Archer	400
	Bal. c/d	3,697		Hornby	700
				Atkins	605
			19	Cash	270
			20	Archer	300
				Atkins	940
				Smart	420
		3,847			3,847
				Bal. b/d	3,697

Fittings account

		£
8	Sampson	1,400

Dobson account

£		£
15 Returns	210	2 Goods	945
21 Bank	735		
	945		945

Gates account

	£
2 Goods	365

Bridges account

£		£
21 Bank	1,422	2 Goods	1,422
	1,422		1,422

Packaging

	£
3 Boxed Ltd	510

Ryan account

	£
2 Goods	850

Sampson account

	£
8 Fittings	1,400

Hornby account

	£
5 Goods	700

Murgatroyd account

	£
6 Goods	212

Archer account

£		£
6 Goods	400	16 Returns	40
20 "	300	21 Bank	660
	700		700

Salaries account

	£
9 Bank	310

Van account

	£
15 Bank	2,300

Atkins account

£		£
6 Goods	605	16 Returns	110
20 "	940	28 Bank	1,000
		Bal. b/d	435
	1,545		1,545
Bal.b/d	435		

Loan S. Small account

	£			£
Bal. c/d	2,000	16	Bank	1,800
		27	"	200
	2,000			2,000
		Bal. b/d		2,000

Rent account

	£
7 Bank	200

Smart account

	£			£
20 Goods	420	22 Bank		420

Electricity account

	£
26 Bank	80

Cash account

	£
19 Sales	270

Norman Coates	Trial Balance		Adjustments		Profit and loss account		Balance Sheet	
	£		£		£		£	
	Dr	Cr	Dr	Cr	Dr	Cr	Dr	Cr
Sales account		3,697				3,697		
Purchases	3,882				3,882			
Packing	510				510			
Stock			1,500	1,500		1,500	1,500	
Gross profit					805			
					5,197	5,197		
Gross profit						805		
Salaries	310		200		510			
Rent	200			100	100			
Electricity	80		70		150			
Net profit					45			45
					805	805		
Sundry debtors								
Murgatroyd	212							
Hornby	700							
Atkins	435							
Rent			100				1,447	
Sundry creditors								
Boxed Ltd		510						
Gates		365						
Sampson		1,400						
Ryan		850						
Electricity				70				
Wages				200				3,395
S. Small loan		2,000						2,000
Capital account		11,000						11,000
Fittings account	1,400						1,400	
Van account	2,300						2,300	
Bank	9,523						9,523	
Cash	270						270	
	19,822	19,822					16,440	16,440

Norman Coates - Profit and loss account for October 19X2

	£	£
Sales		3,697
Less: Cost of sales		
Purchases	4,392	
Less Closing stock	1,500	2,892
Gross profit		805
Less: Salaries	510	
Rent	100	
Electricity	150	760
Net profit carried to Capital account		45

Balance Sheet as at 31 October 19X2

Capital introduced	11,000
Add net profit for month	45
	11,045
Loan - S. Small	2,000
Sundry creditors	3,395
	16,440
Represented by:	
Fittings	1,400
Motor van	2,300
	3,700
Stock	1,500
Debtors	1,447
Bank	9,523
Cash	270
	16,440

Note: In the suggested solutions for both Questions 3 and 4 the individual expense and sale accounts have not been closed off to the Profit and loss account as this is not likely to be done in practice. However, at this stage it is useful to demonstrate closing off the accounts for the sake of completeness.

QUESTION 5

P. Earnshaw

	Trial Balance		Adjustments		Profit and loss account		Balance Sheet	
	Dr £	Cr £	Dr £	Cr £	Dr £	Cr £	Dr £	Cr £
Purchases	67,800				67,800			
Sales		112,960				112,960		
Stock	16,540		13,436	13,436	16,540	13,436	13,436	
Gross profit					42,056			
					126,396	126,396		
Gross profit						42,056		
Postage and Telephone	912			35	877			
Motor expenses	1,596		121		1,717			
Salaries	17,456				17,456			
Sundry expenses	332		95		427			
Rent	1,560				1,560			
Rates	620			90	530			
Bad debts			624		624			
Net profit					18,865			18,865
					42,056	42,056		
Debtors	28,792			624				
Rates prepaid			90					
Telephone prepaid			35				28,293	
Creditors		16,696						
Sundry expenses				95				
Motor expenses				121				16,912
Premises	30,000						30,000	
Motor vehicles	9,400						9,400	
Fixtures & fittings	4,480						4,480	
Bank overdraft		1,832						1,832
Drawings	15,400						15,400	
Capital		63,400						63,400
	194,888	194,888					101,009	101,009

P. Earnshaw - Profit and loss account for the year ended 31 May 19X5

		£	£
Sales			112,960
Less	Cost of Sales		
	Stock 1 June 19X4	16,540	
	Purchases	67,800	
	Goods available for sale	84,340	
	Less stock 31 May 19X5	13,436	70,904
Gross profit			42,056
Less:	Salaries	17,456	
	Rent	1,560	
	Rates	530	
	Postages and telephone	877	
	Sundry expenses	427	
	Motor expenses	1,717	
	Bad debts	624	23,191
Net profit carried to Capital account			18,865

Balance sheet as at 31 May 19X5

	£	£
Capital as at 1 June 19X4		63,400
Add net profit for year to 31 May 19X5		18,865
		82,265
Less drawings for year		15,400
		66,865
Sundry creditors	16,912	
Bank overdraft	1,832	18,744
		85,609
Represented by:		
Premises at cost	30,000	
Motor vehicles	9,400	
Fixtures and fittings	4,480	43,880
Stock	13,436	
Sundry debtors and prepayments	28,293	41,729
		85,609

QUESTION 6

C. Hopley

	Trial Balance		Adjustments		Profit and loss account		Balance Sheet	
	Dr £	Cr £	Dr £	Cr £	Dr £	Cr £	Dr £	Cr £
Sales		153,000				153,000		
Purchases	122,400				122,400			
Stock	14,000		13,200	13,200	14,000	13,200	13,200	
Gross profit					29,800			
					166,200	166,200		
Gross profit						29,800		
Wages & salaries	13,498		116		13,614			
Rent and rates	1,650				1,650			
Lighting and heating	642				642			
Insurances	168			40	128			
Printing & Stationery	180				180			
Motor expenses	1,350				1,350			
General expenses	4,400				4,400			
Bad debts	1,132				1,132			
Provision for bad debts			200		200			
Net profit					6,504			6,504
					29,800	29,800		
Trade debtors	16,300							
Insurance prepaid			40					
Provision - debts		300		200			15,840	
Trade creditors		13,228						
Wages				116				13,344
Furniture and fittings	1,450						1,450	
Motor vans	4,160						4,160	
Bank balance	1,930						1,930	
Capital		20,932						20,932
Drawings	4,200						4,200	
	187,460	187,460					40,780	40,780

C. Hopley - Profit and loss account for the year ended 31 December 19X1

	£	£
(a) Sales		153,000
Less: Cost of sales		
Purchases	122,400	
Stock 1 January 19X1	14,000	
Goods available for sale	136,400	
Less Stock 31 December 19X2	13,200	123,200
Gross profit		29,800
Less: Wages and salaries	13,614	
Rent and rates	1,650	
Lighting and heating	642	
Insurances	128	
Printing and stationery	180	
Motor expenses	1,350	
General expenses	4,400	
Bad debts	1,132	
Increase in provision for doubtful debts	200	23,296
Net profit carried to Capital account		6,504

Balance Sheet as at 31 December 19X1

	£	£
(b) Capital as at 1 January 19X1		20,932
Add net profit for year to 31 December 19X1		6,504
		27,436
Less drawings		4,200
		23,236
Sundry creditors		13,344
		36,580
Represented by:		
Furniture and fittings		1,450
Motor vans		4,160
		5,610
Stock	13,200	
Sundry debtors and Prepayments	15,840	
Bank balance	1,930	30,970
		36,580

QUESTION 7

		£	£
(a)	Stock at 31 December 19X4		
	Purchases during year		39,300
	Less cost of goods sold		33,600
			5,700

		£
(b)	Sales on credit during year	44,800
	Less cash received from trade debtors	39,936
	Trade debtors at 31 December 19X4	4,864

		£
(c)	Purchases on credit during year	39,300
	Less payments made to trade creditors	32,408
		6,892

		£	£
(d)	Initial bank deposit		6,000
	Received - Trade debtors		39,936
			45,936
	Less paid out - Rent and fittings, etc.	3,000	
	Business expenses	5,500	
	Trade creditors	32,408	
	Drawings	4,400	45,308
	Balance at bank 31 December 19X4		628

(e)

Business Expenses account

19X4	£	19X4	£
31 Dec Bank	5,500	31 Dec Amounts prepaid c/d	144
31 " Amounts due c/d	212	31 " Transfer to profit and loss account	5,568
	5,712		5,712
19X5		19X5	
1 Jan Bal. - prepaid b/d	144	1 Jan Bal. due b/d	212

(f) H. Latham - Profit and loss account for year ended 31 December 19X4

	£	£
Sales		44,800
Less Cost of sales		33,600
Gross profit		11,200
Less Business expenses		5,568
Net profit carried to Capital account		5,632

(g) Balance Sheet as at 31 December 19X4

	£	£
Capital introduced		6,000
Add net profit for year		5,632
		11,632
Less drawings for year		4,400
		7,232
Sundry creditors trade	6,892	
expense	212	7,104
		14,336
Represented by:		
Fittings and furniture		3,000
Stock		5,700
Trade debtors	4,864	
Prepayments	144	5,008
Balance at bank		628
		14,336

Chapter 4

QUESTION 1

		£	£
(a)	Purchase of new van		
	Dr New van account	2,800	
	Cr Bank or cash account		2,400
	Cr Asset disposal account	_____	400
		2,800	2,800

Dr Asset disposal account   260

Cr Old van account   260

Transfer of net written down value
of old van to asset disposal

(Note: In the absence of both gross asset and depreciation figures, the net figure can be used in this way.)

	£	£
Dr Asset disposal account	140	
Cr Profit and loss account		140

Transfer of the 'gain' on disposal to
the Profit and loss account

(b) This would normally be regarded as an expense, but the expenditure could be
regarded as relating to more than one period. It would then be treated as an
expense over the relevant number of years (usually only a few) and a part transferred to the Profit and loss account of each year.

(c) The purchase of three old cars for spares would be regarded in exactly the same
way as the purchase of any spares and any unused parts would be included in the
year-ending stock.

(d) All labour time engaged on making the storage bin would be regarded as capital.
The scrap sale value, if any, would also be regarded as capital and the credit
would be an offset or original metal purchase as the external sale as scrap
would have been.

Thus the book-keeping would be

Dr Storage bins account ⎫	with value of men's time
Cr Wages account ⎭	spent on construction.

Dr Storage bins account ⎫	with scrap value of
Cr Metal purchases account ⎭	metal used.

Any other expenses used would require similar treatment. The treatment is suggested as an asset of some future service potential is recognized.

(e) The gross cost of the new calculators would be recognized as capital and any allowances for the mechanical adding machines would be taken into account in arriving at the net gain or loss on their disposal. The calculators are presumed to have future potential service as assets.

(f) Repainting would normally be regarded as an expense of the year in which it was incurred, but, as in (b) above, a case might be advanced to regard some of the expenditure as relating to more than one accounting period.

(g) The service potential of the new heating system would be recognized and the outlay of £3,200 would be treated as capital expenditure. The receipt of £850 for scrap would be treated as a 'gain' on disposal of the old system.

(h) The long-term potential service of the fire escape would mean the recognition of the cost of £985 as acquisition of an asset.

QUESTION 2

(a) Presentation of data relevant to economic life

Life of asset in years	1	2	3	4
	£	£	£	£
Cost of acquisition	8,000	8,000	8,000	8,000
Repair costs	200	200	200	200
		850	850	850
			1,200	1,200
				1,300
Total cost	8,200	9,050	9,250	10,550
Disposal value	3,500	2,800	2,000	0
	4,700	6,250	7,250	10,550
Average annual ÷	1	2	3	4
	4,700	3,125	2,417	2,638

From the above, it can be seen that a three-year life cycle would involve least cost.

(b) With an incremental repair expense as large as this, it may be thought appropriate to use a depreciation method which allocates a large part of the cost to the earlier years. Thus for three years, it is suggested that a Sum of Years Digits method be adopted.

Thus the charge to the Profit and loss for each of the three years would be:

S.Y.D. = (1 + 2 + 3) = 6. Depreciable Cost £8,000 - £2,000 = £6,000

Year	1		2		3	
		£		£		£
Depreciation	(3/6)	3,000	(2/6)	2,000	(1/6)	1,000
		200		850		1,200
		3,200		2,850		2,200

QUESTION 3

(a) The annual provision for depreciation under the straight line method would be calculated thus:

$$\frac{12,000 - 1,500}{5} = £2,100 \text{ per annum}$$

Each year the provision would be credited with £2,100 and the income statement debited with the same amount.

(b) The decreasing balance method would require the following calculation to determine the annual rate to be applied to the written down balance

$$r = 1 - 5\sqrt{\frac{1,500}{12,000}}$$

$$r = 1 - 5\sqrt{0.125}$$

$$r = 1 - 0.66 = 0.34 = 34\%$$

	£	£
Cost of Asset		12,000
Less depreciation year 1 .34 × 12,000 =		4,080
Written down value end of year 1		7,920
Less depreciation year 2 .34 × 7,920 =		2,693
Written down value end of year 2		5,227
Less depreciation year 3 .34 × 5,227 =		1,777
Written down value end of year 3		3,450
Less depreciation year 4 .34 × 3,450 =		1,173
Written down value end of year 4		2,277
Less depreciation year 5 .34 × 2,227 =		774
Closing value = scrap value		1,503

(c) Sum of Years Digit method

$$\underline{5 + 4 + 3 + 2 + 1} = 15 = \text{Sum of years digits}$$

		£
First year Cost of asset		12,000
Less depreciation year 1 (5/15 × £10,500)	=	3,500
Written down value end of year 1		8,500
Less depreciation year 2 (4/15 × £10,500)	=	2,800
Written down value end of year 2		5,700
Less depreciation year 3 (3/15 × £10,500)	=	2,100
Written down value end of year 3		3,600
Less depreciation year 4 (2/15 × £10,500)	=	1,400
Written down value end of year 4		2,200
Less depreciation year 5 (1/15 × £10,500)	=	700
Written down value end of year 5 = scrap		1,500

(d) Production usage

Total capacity 2,500 + 5,000 + 3,000 + 3,000 + 1,500 = 15,000

		£
Cost of Asset		12,000
Less depreciation year 1 $\left(\frac{2,500}{15,000} \times £10,500\right)$	=	1,750
Written down value end of year 1		10,250
Less depreciation year 2 $\left(\frac{5,000}{15,000} \times £10,500\right)$	=	3,500
Written down value end of year 2		6,750
Less depreciation year 3 $\left(\frac{3,000}{15,000} \times £10,500\right)$	=	2,100
Written down value end of year 3		4,650
Less depreciation year 4 $\left(\frac{3,000}{15,000} \times £10,500\right)$	=	2,100
Written down value end of year 4		2,550
Less depreciation year 5 $\left(\frac{1,500}{15,000} \times £10,500\right)$	=	1,050
Written down value end of year 5		1,500

QUESTION 4

Machine tools account

19X4		£	19X5	£
Jan. 1 Cash		16,000	Jan. 1 Asset disposal account	8,000
19X5				
Jan. 1 Cash		11,000	Dec.31 Balance c/d	19,000
		27,000		27,000
19X6				
Jan. 1 Balance b/d		19,000		

Reprographic machine account

19X4	£		£
Jan. 1 Cash	4,000		

Provision for depreciation account - machine tools

19X5	£	19X4	£
Jan. 1 Asset disposal account	2,000	Dec.31 Profit and loss account	4,000
		19X5	
Dec.31 Balance c/d	6,625	Dec.31 Profit and loss account	
		(25% × (£8,000 - £2,000))	
		+ (25% × £11,000) =	4,625
	8,625		8,625
		19X6	
		Jan. 1 Balance b/d	6,625

Provision for depreciation account - reprographic machine

19X5	£	19X4	£
Dec.31 Balance c/d	1,200	Dec.31 Profit and loss account	600
		19X5	
		Dec.31 Profit and loss account	600
	1,200		1,200
		19X5	
		Dec.31 Balance b/d	1,200

Asset disposal account

19X5		£	19X5		£
Jan. 1	Machine tools account	8,000	Jan. 1	Provision for depreciation	2,000
			Jan. 1	Cash - proceeds of sale	4,500
			Dec.31	Loss - Profit and loss account	1,500
		8,000			8,000

(2) Points to be raised in discussion:

    (i) depreciation does not necessarily ensure the availability of cash within the business to secure a replacement;

    (ii) depreciation based on historic cost will only cover original cost; any price change would need some foresight of replacement cost if it was to be provided by restricting the amount of net profit distributable.

QUESTION 5

Machinery account

19X1		£	19X3		£
Jan. 1	Cash	60,000	June 30	Asset disposal account	20,000
19X3			Dec. 31	Balance c/d	62,000
Jan. 1	Cash	22,000			
		82,000			82,000
19X4					
Jan. 1	Balance b/d	62,000			

Provision for depreciation account - machinery

19X2		£	19X1		£
Dec.31	Balance c/d	21,600	Dec.31	Profit and loss a/c	12,000
			19X2		
			Dec.31	Profit and loss a/c	9,600
		21,600			21,600
19X3			**19X3**		
June 30	Asset disposal	7,200	Jan. 1	Balance b/d	21,600
			19X3		
Dec.31	Balance c/d	23,920	Dec.31	Profit and loss a/c (20% ×(£40,000-£14,400)) + (20% × £22,000) =	9,520
		31,120			31,120
			19X4		
			Jan. 1	Balance b/d	23,920

40

Asset disposal account

19X3		£	19X3		£
June 30	Machinery account	20,000	June 30	Provision for depreciation	7,200
			June 30	Cash from sale	8,000
			Dec. 31	Loss on disposal - Profit and loss account	4,800
		20,000			20,000

(2) Points to be made:

(i) In determining profit, depreciation is not an optimal charge, so profit could not exist in this case.

(ii) The size of the amount set aside for depreciation provision may vary depending on the view of the life of the asset and the method of allocation adopted.

QUESTION 6

J. Martin - Summary cash/bank account

19X0		£	19X0		£
Jan. 1	Capital	70,000	Dec. 31	Fixed assets	36,000
Dec.31	Received	106,938	Dec. 31	Materials	84,722
			Dec. 31	Wages	37,168
			Dec. 31	General expenses	5,838
			Dec. 31	Drawings - J. Martin	8,234
			Dec. 31	Balance c/d	4,976
		176,938			176,938
19X1					
Jan. 1	Balance b/d	4,976			

J. Martin - Profit and loss account for year ended 31 December, 19X0

		£	£
Revenues Earned			115,484
Less Expenses - Materials used		86,038	
Wages		37,752	
Depreciation		3,600	
General Expenses		5,838	
		133,228	
Less Work-in-progress		25,362	107,866
Surplus carried to capital account			7,618

41

Balance Sheet as at 31 December 19X0

	£	£
Capital introduced		70,000
Add surplus for year		7,618
		77,618
Less drawings for year		8,234
		69,384
Creditors		7,908
		77,292
Fixed assets - at cost		36,000
Less provision for depreciation		3,600
		32,400
Stock - Raw materials	6,008	
Work-in-progress	25,362	
Debtors	8,546	
Bank and cash	4,976	
		77,292

J. Martin	Trial Balance		Adjustments		Profit and loss account		Balance Sheet	
	Dr	Cr	Dr	Cr	Dr	Cr	Dr	Cr
	£	£	£	£	£	£	£	£
Materials	84,722		7,324	6,008	86,038			
Wages	37,168		584		37,752			
Depreciation			3,600		3,600			
General expenses	5,838				5,838			
Work-in-progress			25,362	25,362		25,362	25,362	
Contract receipts		106,938		8,546		115,484		
Surplus					7,618			7,618
					140,846	140,846		
Fixed assets	36,000						36,000	
Provision for depreciation				3,600				3,600
Capital		70,000						70,000
Drawings	8,234						8,234	
Bank & cash	4,976						4,976	
Creditors								
Materials				7,324				
Wages				854				7,908
Stock materials			6,008				6,008	
Debtors			8,546				8,546	
	176,938	176,938					89,126	89,126

Notes

		£	£
(i)	Calculation of work-in-progress		
	Rush Homes Ltd - Materials	17,584	
	Wages	3,528	
	Expenses (25% × £3,528)	882	21,994
	Poole Villas Materials	10,288	
	Wages	2,464	
	Expenses (25% × £2,464)	616	
		13,368	
	Less cash received	10,000	3,368
			25,362

		£	£
(ii)	Debtors - Gorse Hill - Invoiced	22,614	
	Less cash	14,068	
		8,546	

			£	
(iii)	Creditors			
	Wages - Incurred		37,752	
	Cash payments		37,168	584
	Materials - Purchased		92,046	
	Payments	120,722		
	Less amount paid for Fixed asset	36,000	84,722	7,324
				7,908

		£
(iv)	Stock - Raw materials - Purchased	92,046
	Used	86,038
		6,008

QUESTION 7

	Trial Balance		Adjustments		Profit and loss account		Balance Sheet	
	Dr £	Cr £	Dr £	Cr £	Dr £	Cr £	Dr £	Cr £
Sales		136,426				136,426		
Purchases	117,354				117,354			
Stock	13,868				13,868			
Stock			7,832	7,832		7,832	7,832	
Gross profit					13,036			
					144,258	144,258		
Gross profit						13,036		
Sales Salaries	10,524				10,524			
Rent and rates	1,676		200	120	1,756			
Lighting & heating	1,982		54		2,036			
Motor expenses	832		78	116	794			
Advertising	2,750				2,750			
Bad debts	152				152			
Provision for doubtful debts	206				206			
Postage and office expenses	958		56		1,014			
Audit and professional charges	86		210		296			
Depreciation –								
Fittings			3,520					
Motors			1,500		5,020			
Net loss						11,512	11,512	
					24,548	24,548		
Capital		67,042						67,042
Drawings	5,000						5,000	
Creditors		14,864						
Rent				200				
Electricity				54				
Motor expenses				78				
Audit fees				210				
Telephone				56				15,462
Debtors	19,200						19,200	
Provision for doubtful debts		754		206				960
Prepayments Rates			120					
Motor expenses			116					236
Fittings	35,200						35,200	
Provision for depreciation		5,292		3,520				8,812
Delivery vans	6,000						6,000	
Provision for depreciation		1,500		1,500				3,000
Bank and cash	10,296						10,296	
	225,878	225,878					95,276	95,276

44

Profit and Loss account for the year ended 31 December 19X6

	£	£
Sales		136,426
Less Cost of sales		
Opening stock	13,868	
Purchases	117,354	
	131,222	
Less Closing stock	7,832	123,390
Gross margin		13,036
Less: Sales salaries	10,524	
Rent and rates	1,756	
Lighting and heating	2,036	
Motor expenses	794	
Advertising	2,750	
Bad debts	152	
Increase in provision for doubtful debts	206	
Postages and office expenses	1,014	
Audit and professional charges	296	
Depreciation - Fittings	3,520	
Delivery vans	1,500	5,020	24,548
Net loss for year carried to capital account		11,512

Balance sheet as at 31 December 19X6

	£	£
Capital as at 1 January 19X6		67,042
Less: Net loss for year ended 31 December 19X6	11,512	
Drawings	5,000	16,512
		50,530
Creditors		15,462
		65,992

Represented by:	£	£	£
Fixed assets	Cost	Depreciation	Net
Fittings and equipment	35,200	8,812	26,388
Delivery vans	6,000	3,000	3,000
	41,200	11,812	29,388
Current assets			
Stock		7,832	
Debtors and prepayments		18,476	
Bank and cash		10,296	36,604
			65,992

QUESTION 8

	Trial Balance Dr £	Cr £	Adjustments Dr £	Cr £	Profit and Loss account Dr £	Cr £	Balance Sheet Dr £	Cr £
Sales		409,600				409,600		
Purchases	335,520			112	335,408			
Stock	29,944		12,972	12,972	29,944	12,972	12,972	
Gross profit					57,220			
					422,572	422,572		
Gross profit						57,220		
Salaries	12,704				12,704			
Travellers' commission	19,850		900		20,750			
Rent	2,700		900		3,600			
Light and heat	950		272		1,222			
Telephone and postage	1,034				1,034			
Stationery and printing	1,474				1,474			
Insurances	608				608			
General expenses	5,122				5,122			
Bad debts	662				662			
Increase in provision for doubtful debts			858		858			
Depreciation			288		288			
Audit charge			400		400			
Net profit					8,498			8,498
					57,220	57,220		
Capital account		48,478						48,478
Drawings	9,776		112				9,888	
Bank	13,208						13,208	
Cash	58						58	
Debtors	38,200						38,200	
Provision for D.D.		288		858				1,146
Office furniture	2,880			288			2,592	
Sundry creditors		16,324						
Rent				900				
Light and heat				272				
Travellers' commission				900				
Audit charges				400				18,796
	474,690	474,690					76,918	76,918

B. Baker. Profit and Loss account for the year ended 30 September 19X3

	£	£
Sales		409,600
Less Cost of sales		
Opening stock	29,944	
Purchases	335,408	
	365,352	
Less Closing stock	12,972	352,380
Gross margin:		57,220
Less Salaries	12,704	
Travellers' commission and expenses	20,750	
Rent	3,600	
Lighting and heating	1,222	
Telephone and postage	1,034	
Stationery and printing	1,474	
Insurances	608	
General expenses	5,122	
Bad debts	662	
Increase on provision for doubtful debts	858	
Decpreciation	288	
Audit charge	400	48,722
Net profit carried to Capital account		8,498

Balance Sheet as at 30 September 19X1		
Capital as at 1 October 19X0		48,478
Add Net profit for year ended 30 September 19X1		8,498
		56,976
Less Drawings		9,888
Capital as at 30 September 19X1		47,088
Creditors		18,796
		65,884

Represented by:		
Office furniture and equipment		2,592
Stock	12,972	
Debtors	37,054	
Bank and cash	13,266	63,292
		65,884

Chapter 5

Cabernet Pinot and Gamay

	Trial Balance		Adjustments		Profit and loss account		Balance Sheet	
	Dr	Cr	Dr	Cr	Dr	Cr	Dr	Cr
	£	£	£	£	£	£	£	£
Sales		168,111				168,111		
Purchases	114,210				114,210			
Stock	18,347		21,234	21,234	18,347	21,234	21,234	
Gross profit					56,788			
					189,345	189,345		
Gross profit						56,788		
Salaries	16,422				16,422			
Rates, light and heat	3,412			500	2,912			
Insurances	318				318			
Advertising	3,685				3,685			
Motor expenses	3,210				3,210			
Repairs and renewals	410				410			
Telephone and postage	586		120		706			
Printing and stationery	214				214			
Depreciation			3,720		3,720			
Bad debts			625		625			
Net profit					24,566			24,566
					56,788			

Account					
Warehouse	27,500			27,500	
Racks and fittings	8,300			8,300	
Provision for depreciation		1,100	1,800		2,900
Delivery vans	7,400			7,400	
Provision for depreciation		1,020	1,480		2,500
Cooling equip.	4,400			4,400	
Provision for depreciation		3,960	440		4,400
S. debtors	8,614		625	7,989	
Prepaid rates			500	500	
S. creditors		7,197	120		7,317
Telephone			120		
Bal. at bank	1,327			1,327	
Cash in hand	183			183	
Capital *		40,000			40,000
Current accounts		11,000			11,000
Drawings	13,850			13,850	
	232,388	232,388		92,683	92,683

* The Capital, Current and Drawings account have been aggregated here for simplicity and the division of net income has been shown in the final accounts.

Profit and loss account for year ended 30 September 19X7

	£	£
Sales		168,111
Less Cost of sales		
Opening stock	18,347	
Purchases	114,210	
	132,557	
Less Closing stock	21,234	111,323
Gross margin		56,788
Less Salaries	16,422	
Rates, light and heating	2,912	
Insurance	318	
Advertising	3,685	
Motor expenses	3,210	
Repairs and renewals	410	
Telephone and postages	706	
Printing and stationery	214	
Depreciation	3,720	
Bad debts	625	32,222
Net profit		24,566
Salary - Pinot	3,500	

Interest on capital - Cabernet	2,700		
Pinot	1,800		
Gamay	1,500	6,000	9,500
Balance of net profit			15,066
Divided: Cabernet 5/10		7,533	
Pinot 2/10		3,013	
Gamay 3/10		4,520	15,066
			0

Balance Sheet as at 30 September 19X7

Fixed Assets	Cost £	Depreciation £	Net £
Warehouse and Shop	27,500	0	27,500
Racks and fittings	8,300	2,900	5,400
Delivery vans	7,400	2,500	4,900
	43,200	5,400	37,800

Current Assets		
Stock	21,234	
Debtors and prepayments	8,489	
Cash at bank	1,327	
Cash in hand	183	
	31,233	

Less: Creditors amounts falling due within one year		
Trade creditors	7,317	
Net current assets		23,916
		61,716

Capital accounts

	Cabernet £	Pinot £	Gamay £	Total £
As at 1 October 19X6	18,000	12,000	10,000	40,000
Current accounts	4,600	3,760	2,640	
Add Interest	2,700	1,800	1,500	
Add Salary	-	3,500	-	
Add Share of net profit	7,533	3,013	4,520	
	14,833	12,073	8,660	
Less Drawings	4,800	5,200	3,850	
Current accounts as at 30 September 19X1	10,033	6,873	4,810	21,716
				61,716

QUESTION 2

Jill and Dora's Boutique

(a) Revised Profit calculation 31 October 19X5

Profit as per Jill's statement

			£
Share of profit	Jill		5,00
	Dora		4,00
Interest of capital	Jill		1,00
	Dora		80
Salary	Dora		3,00
			13,80

Adjustments - profit	Decrease	Increase	
Stock - overvalued (1)	280		
Bank charges (2)	140		
Depreciation	900		
Purchases	740		
Rates prepaid		160	
Loan interest	300		
	2,360	160	2,20
Revised net profit			11,60
Interest on capital			
Jill 10,000 @ 10%		1,000	
Dora 4,000 @ 10%	400		
4,000 @ 10% ÷ 2 =	200	600	
Salary - Dora		2,800	4,40
			7,20
Divided Jill 5/9 × 7,200 =		4,000	
Dora 4/9 × 7,200 =		3,200	7,20
			0

Notes (1) The figure expected to be realized is regarded as the lowest.
(2) The Bank balance will be adjusted as it must be assumed the
bank figure is as per the cash book.

(b) Current Accounts

		Jill £		Dora £
Balance per original balance sheet		1,960		1,44
Adjustments				
Amounts over-credited				
Salary			-200	
Interest			-200	
Profit		-1,000	-800	1,20
		960		24

52

(c) Balance Sheet as at 31 October 19X5

Fixed assets	Cost	Depreciation		
	£	£	£	£
Shop	16,000	3,120	12,880	
Fittings	10,000	5,000	5,000	
	26,000	8,120		17,880

Current assets				
Stocks			3,900	
Trade debtors			4,220	
Prepayments			440	
Cash in hand			320	
			8,880	

Less: Creditors amounts falling due
within one year

Bank overdraft		680		
Trade creditors and accruals				
(2,400 + 680)		2,580		
			3,260	

Net current assets				5,620
				23,500

Creditors amounts falling due after more than one year

Loans plus accrued interest				4,300
				19,200

Capital accounts	Jill	Dora	Total
	£	£	£
Balance	10,000	8,000	18,000
Current accounts			
Balances	960	240	1,200
			19,200

(d) This final section has been added to draw students' attention to the fact that
interest paid to partners and any salary paid to a partner are really ways of
dividing the net profit between themselves.

QUESTION 3

(a) The value of goodwill is Frank Graine's business is to be found by the following:
Total purchase price lews net tangible assets.
The net (revised) tangible assets of Frank Graine are: (old values in brackets).

	£	£
Freehold warehouse	13,500	(8,210)
Warehouse Fittings	1,250	(1,500)
Motor Vans	6,000	(6,350)
Fixed Assets	20,750	(16,060)
Current Assets		
Stock	17,731	(18,621)
Debtors	11,190	(12,190)
Bank balance *	3,547	(3,547)
	32,468	(34,358)
Less Current liabilities	7,950	(7,640)
	24,518	(26,718)
	45,268	(42,778)

* When taking over the business of a sole trader it is not usual to take over any
cash or bank balances. However, since the problem is silent on the point two
solutions are offered which may be advanced by students.
(i) without the bank balance
Net tangible assets = £45,268 - £3,547 = £41,721
Goodwill = Value of offer = 15,000 × £3 = 45,000 - 41,721 = £3,279
(ii) £45,268 - £45,000 = Negative goodwill of £268
i.e. on that basis the net tangible assets appear to be overvalued.

(b) The share premium in Morgain Ltd's accounts will be
£45,000 - £15,000 = £30,000.
The book-keeping would be summarized

	£	£
Various net assets taken over	45,000	
Share capital account (Ordinary)		15,000
Share premium account		30,000
	45,000	45,000

(c) Schedule of Assets and Liabilities taken over by Morgain Ltd

	(i) Without Bank £	(ii) With Bank £
as per statement in (a) above	41,721	42,268
Goodwill	3,279	- 268
	45,000	45,000

54

(d) The offer to Frank Graine is

Nominal value of shares × market price per share = market value

£15,000   ×   £3   = £45,000

QUESTION 4 OWEN & ARTHUR

The problem requires three stages

  (i) to prepare a Profit and Loss Account in the normal way for the partnership;

  (ii) to adjust the values of the partnership assets in order to determine the value of goodwill;

  (iii) incorporate the adjustments into the new company's balance sheet.

(a) Owen and Arthur - Profit and Loss Account for year ended 30 September 19X7

	£	£
Sales		85,962
Less: Cost of sales		
Opening stock	4,632	
Purchases	58,124	
	62,756	
Less Closing stock	5,321	57,435
Gross profit		28,527
Less: Wages	2,650	
Rates and insurance	1,120	
Electricity	934	
Postages and telephone	734	
Advertising and stationery	750	
Accountancy fees	250	
Motor expenses	1,648	
Depreciation - Fittings 250		
Delivery vans 760	1,010	9,096
Net Profit for year		19,431
Interest on capital - Owen	900	
Arthur	600	1,500
		17,931
Division of balance of net profit:		
Owen (6/10)	10,759	
Arthur (4/10)	7,172	17,931
		0

(b) Revised Balance Sheet - Owen and Arthur as at 30 September 19X7

			£	£
Fixed Assets				
Goodwill				2,985

	Cost	Depreciation		
	£	£		
Shop	16,000	-	16,000	
Fittings	2,500	1,750	750	
Delivery van	3,800	2,280	1,520	
	22,300	4,030	18,270	
Current Assets				
Stock			5,321	
Debtors and prepayments			3,254	
Bank and cash			6,869	
			15,444	
Less Creditors amounts falling due within one year			1,699	
Net current assets				13,745
				35,000

	Owen	Arthur	Total
Capital at 1 October 19X6			
Current accounts at 1 October 19X6	9,000	6,000	15,000
Add Interest on capital	1,210	462	
Share of net profit	900	600	
*Share of revalued assets	10,759	7,172	
	4,011	2,674	
Less Drawings during year	16,880	10,908	
	4,130	3,658	
	12,750	7,250	20,000
			35,000

* Calculation of revised values

	Owen	Arthur	Total
Share of increase in shop value	2,220	1,480	3,700
Share in Goodwill	1,791	1,194	2,985
	4,011	2,674	6,685

Goodwill = £35,000 - £32,015, the old net asset value after the property
revaluation

= £2,985

(c) The number of shares which Owen and Arthur each receive is the sum of their capital and current accounts.

	Owen £	Arthur £	Total £
Capital account	9,000	6,000	
Current account	12,750	7,250	
	21,750	13,250	35,000

(d) Waverton (Sports) Ltd Balance Sheet as at 1 October 19X7

			£
Fixed Assets			
Goodwill			2,985

	Cost £	Depreciation £	£
Fixed Assets			
Freehold shop	16,000	-	16,000
Fittings	750	-	750
Delivery van	1,520	-	1,520
	18,270		18,270
Current Assets			
Inventory		5,321	
Debtors and prepayments		3,254	
Balance at bank and cash in hand		6,869	
		15,444	
Less Creditors amounts falling due within one year		1,699	13,745
			35,000
			£
Capital and reserves			
Called up share capital			35,000

QUESTION 5

Portlin Ltd   Balance Sheet as at 30 June 19X4

Fixed assets

	Cost	Depreciation		
	£000	£000	£000	
Freehold land and buildings	1,600	-	1,600	
Plant and machinery	3,748	1,208	2,540	
Motor vehicles	1,860	480	1,380	
	7,208	1,688		5,520

Investments at cost		740
Current assets		
Stocks	3,720	
Trade debtors	1,776	
Cash in hand	84	
	5,580	
Less: Creditors amounts falling due		
within one year		
Bank overdraft	1,360	
Trade creditors	928	
Accruals	120	
Proposed dividends	380	
	2,788	
Net current assets		2,792
Total assets less current liabilities		9,052
Creditors amounts falling due after one year		
10% Debenture		1,700
		7,352
Capital and reserves		
Called up share capital		4,000
Share premium account		712
General reserve		1,000
Profit and loss account		1,640
		7,352

58

QUESTION 6

R. Quillan Ltd Profit and Loss Account for the year ended 31 March 19X5

	£000	£000	£000
Sales			59,500
Less Cost of sales			35,100
			24,400
Gross margin			
Less:			
Wages and salaries		6,306	
Administration expenses		4,500	
Advertising		475	
Motor expenses		7,450	
Depreciation - Motors	650		
Fixtures and fittings	55	705	
Audit fee		175	
Debenture interest		160	
Increase in provision for doubtful debts		175	19,996
Net profit for year			4,404
Provision for corporation tax			1,800
			2,604
Dividends - Preference		525	
Proposed ordinary at the rate of 7%		700	1,225
Retained profit for year			1,379
Balance of retained profit brought forward			4,545
Retained profit carried forward			5,924

Note. Since the fees of £6,000 for the Chairman are referred to as 'additional' it
is presumed that his other emoluments are included in 'Wages and salaries'.
The £6,000 is added here. This is not meant to be taken as a demonstration
of compliance with any particular disclosure requirements.

Balance sheet as at 31 March 19X5

Fixed assets

	Cost	Depreciation		
	£000	£000	£000	£000
Freehold land and buildings	8,500	-	8,500	
Fixtures and fittings	3,230	1,170	2,060	
Motor vehicles	1,960	695	1,265	
	13,690	1,865		11,825

Current assets

Stocks		10,300
Trade debtors (16,995 - 900)		16,095
Cash at bank and in hand (5,715 + 95)		5,810
		32,205

Less: Creditors amounts falling due within one year

Trade creditors	9,106	
Proposed dividend	700	
		9,806

Net current assets	22,399
Total assets less current liabilities	34,224

Creditors amounts falling due after one year

8% Debenture	2,000

Provision for liabilities and charges

Corporation tax	1,800	
		3,800
		30,424

Capital and reserves

Called up share capital	20,000
General reserve	4,500
Profit and loss account	5,924
	30,424

QUESTION 7

Linthal Limited   Profit and Loss Account for the year ended 30 September 19X0

	£	£
Sales		143,690
Less Cost of sales		
Opening stock	6,390	
Purchases	110,430	
	116,820	
Less Closing stock	9,430	107,390
Gross margin		36,300
Less: Rent and rates (£5,500 - £750)	4,750	
Lighting and heating	960	
Telephone and postages (£930 + £130)	1,060	
Salaries	14,000	
Directors' fees	6,000	
Advertising	1,400	
Motor expenses	2,340	

	£	£	£
Depreciation - Delivery vans	1,200		
Fixtures and fittings	600	1,800	32,310

	£
Net profit for the year	3,990
Retained profit brought forward	8,700
	12,690
Proposed ordinary dividend at rate of 20%	4,000
Retained profit carried forward	8,690

Balance Sheet as at 30 September 19X0

Fixed assets	Cost	Depreciation		
	£	£	£	£
Fixtures and fittings	7,400	3,200	4,200	
Motor vehicles	10,800	4,440	6,360	
	18,200	7,640		10,560

Current assets	£
Stocks	9,430
Trade debtors and prepayments	11,960
Cash at bank	8,350
	29,740

Less: Creditors amounts falling due within one year		
Trade creditors	7,610	
Proposed dividend	4,000	11,610

Net current assets	18,130
	28,690

Capital and reserve	£
Called up share capital	20,000
Profit and loss account	8,690
	28,690

QUESTION 8

Bargemon Limited

(1)

Summarized bank account 19X1

(a)				
Balance b/d	19,722	Paid to creditors	362,432
Received from debtors	460,674	Fixed assets	12,844
Disposal of fixed assets	1,000	Dividend 19X0	40,000
Balance overdrawn c/d	1,290	Business expenses	67,410
	482,686		482,686
		Balance b/d	1,290

Summarized sundry debtors 19X1

(b)				
Balance b/d	103,046	Returns	5,066
Sales	526,016	Bank	460,674
		Bad debts	1,592
		Contra-creditors	42,000
		Balance c/d	119,370
	629,062		629,062
Balance b/d	119,370		

Summarized sundry creditors

(c) Returns	4,008	Balance b/d	82,558
Bank	362,432	Purchases	426,174
Contra-debtors	42,000		
Balance c/d	100,292		
	508,732		508,732
		Balance b/d	100,292

Fixed assets account

(d) Balance b/d	221,352	Asset disposal account	10,758
Bank	12,844	Balance c/d	223,438
	234,196		234,196
Balance b/d	223,438		

Provision for depreciation of fixed assets account

(e) Asset disposal account	9,182	Balance b/d	82,412
Balance c/d	97,758	Profit and Loss Account	24,528
	106,940		106,940
		Balance b/d	97,758

Asset disposal account

(f) Fixed assets	10,758	Provision for depreciation	9,182
		Bank	1,000
		Loss - Profit and Loss a/c	576
	10,758		10,758

Provision for doubtful debts account

(g) Balance c/d	2,458	Balance b/d	2,216
		Profit and Loss Account	242
	2,458		2,458
		Balance b/d	2,458

Inventory account

(h) Balance b/d	128,154	Purchase returns	4,008
Purchases	426,174	Profit and Loss Account	392,846
		Balance c/d	157,474
	554,328		554,328
Balance b/d	157,474		

Note The amount transferred to the Profit and Loss Account is arrived at by taking the cost of sales sections from the cost of stock sold (£396,676 - £3,830).

(i) Balance - prepayments b/d	1,086	Balance - accruals b/d	3,446
Bank	67,410	Prepayments 19X1 c/d	1,164
Accruals 19X1	3,798	Profit and Loss Account	67,684
	72,294		72,294
Balance prepayments b/d	1,164	Balance accruals b/d	3,798

(2) Profit and Loss Account for year ended 31 December 19X1

	£	£
Sales		520,950
Less Cost of sales		392,846
Gross profit		128,104
Less:		
Business expenses	67,684	
Depreciation	24,528	
Loss on disposal of fixed assets	576	
Increase in provision for doubtful debts	242	
Bad debts	1,952	94,982
Net profit		33,122
Proposed dividend		30,000
		3,122
Retained profit brought forward 19X0		62,728
Retained profit carried forward 19X1		65,850

QUESTION 8

Balance Sheet as at 31 December 19X1

	Cost	Depreciation	
	£	£	£
Fixed assets	223,438	97,758	125,680

Current assets		£	£
Stocks			157,474
Trade debtors (less provision for doubtful debt £2,458)			116,912
Prepayments			1,164
			275,550

Less: Creditors amounts falling due within one year			
Bank overdraft	1,290		
Trade creditors	100,292		
Proposed dividend	30,000		
Accruals	3,798		
		135,380	

Net current assets	140,170
	265,850

Capital and reserve	£
Called up share capital	200,000
Profit and loss account	65,850
	265,850

QUESTION 9

Ravel Limited
All figures are in £000s.

(1)

Bank account

Sundry debtors 19X3	702	Balance o/d b/d	12
Share capital - ordinary	60	Fixed assets	51
Sale of fixed assets	9	Sundry creditors	339
		Wages and salaries	162
		Administration expenses	30
		Selling and distribution expenses	33
		Corporation tax	27
		Ordinary dividend	24
		Balance 19X4 c/d	93
	771		771
Balance 19X4 b/d	93		

Sundry debtors

Balance 19X3 b/d	114	Bank	702
Sales	732	Returns	18
		Bad debts	6
		Balance 19X4 c/d	120
	846		846
Balance 19X4 b/d	120		

Sales account

Sundry debtors (returns)	18	Sundry debtors	732
Profit and Loss Account	714		
	732		732

Purchases account

Sundry creditors	441	Sundry creditors (returns)	9
		Profit and Loss Account	432
	441		441

Administration expenses account

Balance - prepayments 19X3 b/d	3	Balance - accruals 19X3 b/d	6
Bank	30	Balance - prepayments 19X3 c/d	6
Balance - accruals 19X4 c/d	4	Profit and Loss Account	25
	37		37
Balance - prepayments 19X4 b/d	6	Balance - prepayments 19X4 c/d	4

Selling and distribution expenses account

Balance - prepayments 19X3 b/d	6	Balance - accruals 19X3 b/d	3
Bank	33	Balance - prepayments 19X4 c/d	4
Balance - accruals 19X4 c/d	8	Profit and Loss Account	40
	47		47
Balance - prepayments 19X4 b/d	4	Balance - accruals 19X4 b/d	8

Corporation Tax account

Bank	27	Balance - provision 19X3 b/d	27
		Profit and Loss account - provision 19X4	26

Ordinary shares dividend account

Bank	24	Balance - provisions 19X3	24
		Profit and Loss account - proposed for 19X4	25

Sundry creditors

Returns	9	Balance 19X3 b/d	60
Bank	339	Purchases	441
Balance 19X4 c/d	153		
	501		501
		Balance 19X4 b/d	153

Fixed assets

Balance 19X3 b/d	270	Asset disposal	27
Bank	51	Balance 19X4 c/d	294
	321		321
Balance 19X4 b/d	294		

Wages and salary account

Bank	162	Balance 19X3 b/d	18
		Profit and Loss Account	144
	162		162

Bad debts account

Sundry debtors	6		

Provision for depreciation - fixed assets account

Asset disposal account	21	Balance 19X3 b/d	90
Balance 19X4 c/d	85	Profit and Loss Account	16
	106		106
		Balance 19X4 b/d	85

Asset disposal account

Fixed assets	27	Provision for depreciation	21
Profit and Loss Account - gain	3	Bank	9
	30		30

Ordinary share capital account

Balance 19X4 c/d	360	Balance 19X3 b/d	300
		Bank	60
	360		360
		Balance 19X4 b/d	360

(2) Trial Balance as at 31 December 19X4

	Dr £	Cr £
Share capital		360
Bank balance	93	
Sundry debtors	120	
Sundry creditors		153
Fixed assets	294	
Provision for depreciation		69
Gain on disposal of asset		3
Sales		714
Purchases	432	
Administration expenses	25	
Administration expenses prepaid and accrued	6	4
Selling and distribution expenses	40	
Selling and distribution expenses prepaid and accrued	4	8
Retained profit		90
Stock	246	
Provision for doubtful debts		9
Wages and salaries account	144	
Bad debts account	6	
	1,410	1,410

Profit and Loss Account for the year ended 31 December 19X4

	£000s	£000s
Sales		714
Less Cost of sales		
Stock 1 January 19X4	246	
Purchases	432	
	678	
Less Closing stock	274	404
Gross profit		310
Less: Wages and salaries	144	
Administration expenses	25	
Selling and distribution expenses	40	
Depreciation	16	
Bad debts	6	
Increase in provision for doubtful debts	1	232
Net profit from operations		78
Gain on disposal of asset		3
		81
Corporation tax		26
		55
Proposed ordinary dividend		25
		30
Retained profit brought forward		90
Retained profit carried forward		120

QUESTION 9

Balance Sheet as at 31 December 19X4

	Cost	Depreciation	
	£000s	£000s	£000s
Fixed assets	294	85	209

	£	£	
Current assets			
Stocks		274	
Trade debtors (less provision for doubtful debts)		110	
Prepayments		10	
Cash at bank		93	
		487	

Less: Creditors amounts falling due within one year			
Trade creditors and accruals	165		
Proposed dividend	25		
		190	

			£000s
Net current assets			297
Total assets less current liabilities			506
Provisions for liabilities and charges Corporation tax			26
			480

			£000s
Capital and reserve			
Called up share capital			360
Profit and loss account			120
			480

Chapter 6

QUESTION 1

Baker Bargains Limited

Debtors control account

19X3		£	19X4			£
Oct. 1	Balance b/d	6,120	Sep. 30	Returns		810
19X4			Sep. 30	Cash		42,150
Sep.30	Sales	47,360	Sep. 30	Discounts allowed		1,440
			Sep. 30	Contra - S. creditors		870
			Sep. 30	Bad debts		380
			Sep. 30	Balance c/d		7,830
		53,480				53,480
19X3						
Oct. 1	Balance b/d	7,830				

Creditors control account

19X4		£	19X3		£
Sep.30	Returns	1,960	Oct. 1	Balance b/d	4,390
Sep.30	Cash	29,600	19X4		
Sep.	Discounts received	967	Sep.30	Purchases	36,114
Sep.30	Contra - S. debtors	870			
Sep.30	Balance c/d	7,107			
		40,504			40,504

QUESTION 2

Debtors control account

19X3		£	19X4		£
July 1	Balance	60,000	June 30	Cash	285,400
19X4			June 30	Discounts allowed	5,600
June 30	Sales	380,000	June 30	Returns	14,000
			June 30	Bad debts	5,000
			June 30	Contra - S.creditors	50,000
			June 30	Balance c/d	80,000
		440,000			440,000
19X4					
July 1	Balance	80,000			

Creditors control account

19X4		£	19X3		£
June 30	Return	3,800	July 1	Balance b/d	32,000
June 30	Cash	122,000	19X4		
June 30	Discount received	2,200	June 30	Purchases	186,000
June 30	Contra	50,000			
	Balance c/d	40,000			
		218,000			218,000
			19X4		
			July 1	Balance b/d	40,000

Provision for doubtful debts account

19X4		£	19X3		£
June 30	Balance c/d	4,000	July 1	Balance b/d	2,000
			19X4		
			June 30	Profit and Loss a/c	2,000
		4,000			4,000
			19X4		
			July 1	Balance b/d	4,000

QUESTION 3

(a)   Debtors control account

19X4		£	19X4			£
Jan. 1	Balance b/d	17,904	Dec. 31	Cash		138,942
Dec.31	Sales	149,506	Dec. 31	Discounts		3,634
			Dec. 31	Balance c/d		24,834
		167,410				167,410
19X4			19X4			
Dec.31	Balance b/d	24,834	Dec. 31	Bank		396
Dec.31	Bank - Spruce	2,346	Dec. 31	Contra - S.creditors	5,792
			Dec. 31	Bad debts		1,280
			Dec. 31	Balance c/d		19,712
		27,180				27,180
19X4						
Dec.31	Balance b/d	19,712				

(b) List of balance extracted from debtors ledger amount to

	£	£
		19,326
Add balances omitted	382	
incorrect balances	400	782
		20,108
Less cash discovered		396
		19,712

(c) Point to be raised in suggested benefits of adopting control accounts
  (i)   Division of labour
  (ii) Continuous check on accuracy of work
  (iii) Continuous check on honesty of clerical staff involved
  (iv) Saving of time in availability of totals.

QUESTION 4

Tullins Groceries

Debtors control account

19X3		£	19X3		£
Jan. 1	Balance b/d	38,541		Balancing figure - cash	403,305
Mar. 24	Sales	428,547	Mar. 24	Balance c/d	63,783
		467,088			467,088
19X4					
Mar. 24	Balance b/d	63,783			

Creditors control account

19X3		£	19X3		£
Mar. 24	Balancing figure - cash	255,189	Jan. 1	Balance b/d	11,115
Mar. 24	Balance c/d	18,828	Mar. 24	Purchases	262,902
		274,017			274,017
			19X3		
			Mar. 24	Balance b/d	18,828

Cash Book (reconstructed in total)

19X3		£		£
Jan. 1	Balance b/d	4,494	Mar. 24 Creditors	255,189
Mar. 24	Debtors	403,305	Mar. 24 Expenses	86,238
			Mar. 24 Vans	7,500
			Mar. 24 Salaries	44,586
			Mar. 24 Dividend	2,520
			Mar. 24 Balance c/d	11,766
		407,799		407,799
19X3				
Mar. 24	Balance b/d	11,766		

If all money had been banked this would have been the balance at the bank. However, the amount at the bank was £7,848 less the cheques subsequently presented at £342 = £7,506

	£
The cash stolen must have been	11,766
	- 7,506
	= 4,260

QUESTION 5

Houlgate Co. Ltd Item No. A312

(a) FIFO Cost of sales and closing stock value

	Units	£
Opening stock 1 October 19X5	250	400
Purchases during month	1,750	3,060
Available for sales	2,000	3,460
Less Closing stock	300	540
Cost of sales for October 19X5	1,700	2,910

Closing stock is most recently acquired

	Units	Price		£
viz.	200	@ £1.85	=	370
+	100	@ £1.80	=	180
				550

(b) LIFO Cost of sales and closing stock value

	Units	£
Opening stock 1 October 19X5	250	400
Purchases during month	1,750	3,060
	2,000	3,460
Less Closing stock	300	485
Cost of sales for October 19X5	1,700	2,975

Closing stock price is assumed to be the earliest purchased or in hand

Units	Price		£
250	@ £1.60	=	400
50	@ £1.70	=	85
300			485

(c) AVCO Cost of sales and closing stock value

	Units	£
Opening stock 1 October 19X5	250	400
Purchases during month	1,750	3,060
Available for sale	2,000	3,460
Less Closing stock	300	519
Cost of sales for October 19X5	1,700	2,941

Closing stock calculated on average cost

$$\text{Unit cost} = \frac{£3,460}{2,000} = £1.73$$

Closing stock is therefore £1.73 × 300 = £519

QUESTION 6

Houlgate Co. Ltd   Item No. A312

FIFO - Perpetual Stock

(a) (i) & (ii)

Date		Received Quantity	Received Unit Price £	Received Value £	Issued Quantity	Issued Unit Price £	Issued Value £	Stock Balance Quantity	Stock Balance Unit Price £	Stock Balance Value £
19X5										
October*1	Balance	250	1.60	400				250	1.60	400
October 5	Sale				200	1.60	320	50	1.60	80
October 8	Purchases	800	1.70	1,360				800	1.70	1,360
	Balance							850		1,440
October 10	Sale				50	1.60	80			
October 10	Sale				650	1.70	1,105	150	1.70	255
October 13	Purchases	400	1.75	700				400	1.75	700
	Balance							550		955
October 15	Sale				150	1.70	255			
October 15	Sale				300	1.75	525	100	1.75	175
October 20	Purchases	350	1.80	630				350	1.80	630
	Balance							450		805
October 23	Sale				100	1.75	175			
October 23	Sale				200	1.80	360	150	1.80	270
October 29	Purchases	200	1.85	370				200	1.85	370
	Balance							350		640
October 30	Sale				50	1.80	90	100	1.80	180
								200	1.85	370
		2,000		3,460	1,700		2,910	300		550

Cost of Sales   = £2,910

Closing stock   = £ 550

This demonstrates the point made in the text that there is no difference in the two values when using the FIFO perpetual method compared to the FIFO periodic stock method.

* For convenience the balance at the start has been treated as received.

LIFO - Perpetual stock
(b) (i) & (ii)

Date		Received Quantity	Received Unit Price £	Received Value £	Issued Quantity	Issued Unit Price £	Issued Value £	Stock Balance Quantity	Stock Balance Unit Price £	Stock Balance Value £
19X5										
October 1	Balance b/d	250	1.60	400				250	1.60	400
October 5	Sale				200	1.60	320	50	1.60	80
October 8	Purchase	800	1.70	1,360				800	1.70	1,360
								850		1,440
October 10	Sale				700	1.70	1,190	50	1.60	80
								100	1.70	170
October 13	Purchase	400	1.75	700				400	1.75	700
								550		950
October 15	Sale				400	1.75	700	50	1.60	80
October 15	Sale				50	1.70	85	50	1.70	85
								100		165
October 20	Purchase	350	1.80	630				350	1.80	630
								450		795
October 23	Sale				300	1.80	540	50	1.60	80
								50	1.70	85
								50	1.80	90
								150		255
October 29	Purchase	200	1.85	370				200	1.85	370
								350		625

Cont'd

| | | Received | | | Issued | | | Stock Balance | |
	Quantity	Unit Price £	Value £	Quantity	Unit Price £	Value £	Quantity	Unit Price £	Value £
October 30 Sale				50	1.85	92.50	50	1.60	80
							50	1.70	85
							50	1.80	90
							150	1.85	277.50
									532.50
	2,000		3,460	1,700		2,927.50	300		

The cost of sales using the LIFO perpetual method can now be seen to be £2,927.50 compared to the figure of £2,975 arrived at in Question 6(b) using the periodic stock method of LIFO with a corresponding change of end of period stock value.

AVCO - Perpetual Stock
(c) (i) & (ii)

Date	Received Quantity	Received Unit Price £	Received Value £	Issued Quantity	Issued Unit Price £	Issued Value £	Stock Balance Quantity	Stock Balance Unit Price £	Stock Balance Value £
October 1 Balance b/d	250	1.60					250	1.60	400
October 5 Sale				200	1.60	320	50	1.60	80
October 8 Purchase	800	1.70	1,360				800	1.70	1,360
Balance							850	1.69	1,440
October 10 Sale				700	1.69	1,183	150	1.69	257
October 13 Purchase	400	1.75	700				400	1.75	700
Balance							550	1.74	957
October 15 Sale				450	1.74	783	100	1.74	174
October 20 Purchase	350	1.80	630				350	1.80	630
Balance							450	1.79	804
October 23 Sale				300	1.79	537	150	1.79	267
October 29 Purchase	200	1.85	370				200	1.85	370
Balance							350	1.84	644
October 30 Sale				50	1.84	92	300	1.84	552
	2,000		3,460	1,700		2,915			

Rounding up adjustment 7

Cost of sales for October 19X5 2,908

The cost of sales using the AVCO perpetual stock method can now be seen to be £2,908 compared to the figure of £2,941 using the AVCO periodic stock method.

QUESTION 7

Portal Home Decorating Co. Ltd
To calculate the amount of stock destroyed

1st step:	calculate cost of sales	£
	Sales to 9 August 19X7	187,200
	Less mark up = $\frac{1}{4}$ on selling	46,800
	Cost of sales =	140,400

2nd step:	calculate the amount of goods available for sale during period:	£
	Opening stock 1 January 19X7	35,612
	Purchases to 9 August 19X7	134,364
	Amount available for sale	169,976
	Less Cost of sales from 1st step	140,400
	Cost of stock destroyed =	29,576

QUESTION 8

Speedwell Engineering Company Ltd

Parts	Quantity	Unit Price Cost	Unit Price Market Value	Cost	Total Market Value	Lower of cost or market
		£	£	£	£	£
Sprockets	2,000	2.00	2.15	4,000	4,000	4,000
Flanges	1,500	3.10	3.00	4,650	4,500	4,500
Gear wheels	3,000	1.60	1.75	4,800	5,250	4,800
Drive chains	1,000	4.30	4.00	4,300	4,000	4,000
Clamps	4,000	1.20	1.25	4,800	5,000	4,800
				22,550	23,050	22,100

Answers (a) £22,550; (b) £22,550; (c) £22,100.

QUESTION 9

Solo Ltd

Note. This question will take students a considerable amount of time to complete if it is set as an assignment in its entirety. It is suggested therefore that (a) and (b)(ii) and (c)(ii) are used.
This omits the tedious arithmetic of the AVCO method and students can be made aware of the volume of work required to use this method in practice.

(a)(i) Gross Profit for 19X6 Periodic stock

FIFO

			£
Sales (2,500 × £5) + (1,700 × £5.50) =			21,850
Less Cost of sales	Units	£	
Opening stock	600	1,260	
Purchases	4,250	10,105	
Available for sale	4,850	11,365	
Closing stock	650	1,685	9,680
Gross profit			12,170

(1) Closing stock =

(200 @ £2.70) + (400 @ £2.55) + (50 @ £2.50) =   £ 1,685

(a)(ii) LIFO

Sales	Units	£	£
Sales	4,200		21,850
Less Cost of sales -			
Available for sale as in (a)(i)	4,800	11,365	
Closing stock	650	1,367.50	9,997.50
			11,852.50

(2) Closing stock =

(600 @ £2.10) + (50 @ £2.15) =   £ 1.367.50

(a)(iii) AVCO

	Units	£	£
Sales	4,200		21,850
Less Cost of sales			
Available for sale as in (a)(i)	4,850	11,365	
Closing stock (3)	650	1,523	9,842
			12,008

(3) Closing stock =

$$\left(650 \times \frac{11,365}{4,850}\right) = £1,523$$

(b)(i) FIFO

As stated in the text there will be no difference in the Gross Profit when the perpetual stock is utilized compared with the use of periodic stock the FIFO cost flow assumptions.

(b)(ii) LIFO - Perpetual stock

Note: (c)(ii) will have to be completed in order to establish the figures for this section.

	Units	£	£
Sales	4,200		21,850
Opening stock	600	1,260	
Purchases	4,250	10,105	
Available for sale	4,850	11,365	
Less Closing stock	650	1,542.50	9,822.50
Gross profit			12,027.50

(b)(iii) AVCO - Perpetual stock

Note: (c)(iii) will have to be completed in order to establish the figures for this section.

	Units	£	£
Sales	4,200		21,850
Less Cost of sale			
Opening stock	600	1,260	
Purchases	4,250	10,105	
Available for sale	4,850	11,365	
Less Closing stock	650	1,657.20	9,707.80
Gross profit			12,142.20

(c)(i) FIFO - Perpetual stock

19X6		Qty	Purchases Unit Price £	Total £	Qty	Sales Unit Price £	Total £	Qty	Balance Unit Price £	Total £
Jan. 1	Stock							600	2.10	1,260
" 8	Sales				400	2.10	840	200	2.10	420
" 23	Purchases	300	2.15	645				300	2.15	645
	Balance							500		1,065
Feb. 2	Sales				200	2.10	420			
					40 (240)	2.15	86	260	2.15	559
" 18	Purchases	700	2.20	1,540				700	2.20	1,540
	Balance							960		2,099
" 23	Sales				260	2.15	559			
					240 (500)	2.20	528	460	2.20	1,012
Mar.14	Purchases	250	2.30	575				250	2.30	575
" 23	Purchases	300	2.35	705				300	2.35	705
	Balance							1,010		2,292
" 27	Sales				200	2.20	440			

			Purchases			Sales			Balance	
		Qty	Unit Price £	Total £	Qty	Unit Price £	Total £	Qty	Unit Price £	Total £
Apr. 3	Sales				260	2.20	572	250	2.30	575
								300	2.35	705
" 10	Purchases	400	2.40	960				400	2.40	960
"	Balance							950		2,240
" 15	Sales				250	2.30	575			
					250	2.35	587.50	50	2.35	117.50
					(500)			400	2.40	960
May 28	Purchases	200	2.30	460				200	2.30	460
June 18	Purchases	200	2.35	470				200	2.35	470
	Balance							850		2,007.50
" 24	Sales				50	2.35	117.50			
					350	2.40	840	50	2.40	120
					(400)			200	2.30	460
								200	2.35	470
July 17	Purchases	300	2.40	720				300	2.40	720
	Balance							750		1,770
Aug. 2	Sales				50	2.40	120			
					200	2.30	460			
					200	2.35	470			
					50	2.40	120	250	2.40	600
					(500)					
" 30	Purchases	600	2.45	1,470				600	2.45	1,470
	Balance							850		2,070
Sept.18	Sales				200	2.40	480	50	2.40	120
" 30	Purchases	400	2.50	1,000				600	2.45	1,470
								400	2.50	1,000
	Balance							1,050		2,590
Oct. 10	Sales				50	2.40	120			
					550	2.45	1,347.50	50	2.45	112.50
					(600)			400	2.50	1,000
Nov. 9	Purchases	400	2.55	1,020				400	2.55	1,020
	Balance							850		2,142.50
Nov. 28	Sales				50	2.45	122.50			
					250	2.50	625	150	2.50	375
					(300)			400	2.55	1,020
Dec. 1	Purchases	200	2.70	540				200	2.70	540
								750		1,935
" 23	Sales				100	2.50	250	50	2.50	125
								400	2.55	1,020
								200	2.70	540
	Balance							650		1,685
	Purchases			10,105						
	Cost of sales						9,680			

84

(c)(ii) LIFO - Perpetual stock

19X6		Purchases Qty	Unit Price £	Total £	Sales Qty	Unit Price £	Total £	Balance Qty	Unit Price £	Total £
Jan.	1 Stock							600	2.10	1,260
"	8 Sales				400	2.10	840	200	2.10	420
"	23 Purchases	300	2.15	645				300	2.15	645
	Balance							500		1,065
Feb.	2 Sales				240	2.15	516	200	2.10	420
								60	2.15	129
Feb.	18 Purchases	700	2.20	1,540				700	2.20	1,540
	Balance							960		2,089
"	23 Sales				500	2.20	1,100	200	2.10	420
								60	2.15	129
								200	2.20	440
Mar.	14 Purchases	250	2.30	575				250	2.30	575
"	23 Purchases	300	2.35	705				300	2.35	705
	Balance							1,010		2,269
"	27 Sales				200	2.35	470	200	2.10	420
								60	2.15	129
								200	2.20	440
								250	2.30	575
								100	2.35	235
	Balance							810		1,799
Apr.	3 Sales				100	2.35	235	200	2.10	420
					160	2.30	368	60	2.15	129
					(260)			200	2.20	440
								90	2.30	207
"	10 Purchases	400	2.40	960				400	2.40	960
	Balance							950		2,156
"	15 Sales				400	2.40	960	200	2.10	420
					90	2.30	207	60	2.15	129
					10	2.20	22	190	2.20	418
					(500)					
May	28 Purchases	200	2.30	460				200	2.30	460
June	18 Purchases	200	2.35	470				200	2.35	470
	Balance							850		1,897
"	24 Sales				200	2.35	470	200	2.10	420
					200	2.30	460	60	2.15	129
					(400)			190	2.20	418

	Purchases Qty	Unit Price £	Total £	Sales Qty	Unit Price £	Total £	Balance Qty	Unit Price £	Total £
July 17 Purchases	300	2.40	720				300	2.40	720
Balance							750		1,687
Aug. 2 Sales				300	2.40	720	200	2.10	420
				190	2.20	418	50	2.15	107.50
				10	2.15	21.50			
				(500)					
" 30 Purchases	600	2.45	1,470				600	2.45	1,470
Balance							850		1,997.50
Sept.18 Sales				200	2.45	490	200	2.10	420
							50	2.15	107.50
							400	2.45	980
" 30 Purchases	400	2.50	1,000				400	2.50	1,000
Balance							1,050		2,507.50
Oct. 10 Sales				200	2.45	490	200	2.10	420
				400	2.50	1,000	50	2.15	107.50
				(600)			200	2.45	490
Nov. 9 Purchases	400	2.55	1,020				400	2.55	1,020
Balance							850		2,037.50
" 28 Sales				300	2.55	765	200	2.10	420
							50	2.15	107.50
							200	2.45	490
							100	2.55	255
Dec. 1 Purchases	200	2.70	540				200	2.70	540
Balance							750		1,812.50
" 23 Sales				100	2.70	270	200	2.10	420
							50	2.15	107.50
							200	2.45	490
							100	2.55	255
							100	2.70	270
Totals			10,105	Cost of sales		9,822.50	650		1,542.50

(c)(iii) AVCO - Perpetual stock

19X6	Purchases Qty	Unit Price £	Total £	Sales Qty	Unit Price £	Total £	Balance Qty	Unit Price £	Total £
Jan. 1 Stock							600	2.10	1,260
" 8 Sales				400	2.10	840	200		420
" 23 Purchases	300	2.15	645				300		645
Balance							500	2.13	1,065

	Purchases Qty	Purchases Unit Price £	Purchases Total £	Sales Qty	Sales Unit Price £	Sales Total £	Balance Qty	Balance Unit Price £	Balance Total £
Feb. 2 Sales				240	2.13	511.20	260		553.80
" 18 Purchases	700	2.20	1,540				700		1,540
Balance							960	2.18	2,093.80
Mar. 23 Sales				500	2.18	1,090	460		1,003.80
" 14 Purchases	250	2.30	575				250		575
" 23 Purchases	300	2.35	705				300		705
Balance							1,010	2.26	2,293.80
" 27 Sales				200	2.26	452			
Apr. 3 Sales				260	2.26	587.60			
Balance							550		1,244.20
" 10 Purchases	400	2.40	960				400		960
Balance							950	2.32	2,204.20
" 15 Sales				500	2.32	1,160	450		1,044.20
May 28 Purchases	200	2.30	460				200		460
June 18 Purchases	200	2.35	470				200		470
Balance							850	2.32	1,974.20
" 24 Sales				400	2.32	928	450		1,046.20
July 17 Purchases	300	2.40	720				300		720
Balance							750	2.35	1,766.20
Aug. 2 Sales				500	2.35	1,180	250		586.20
" 30 Purchases	600	2.45	1,470				600		1,470
Balance							850	2.42	2,056.20
Sept. 18 Sales				200	2.42	484	650		1,572.20
" 30 Purchases	400	2.50	1,000				400		1,000
Balance							1,050	2.45	2,572.20
Oct. 10 Sales				600	2.45	1,470	450		1,102.20
Nov. 9 Purchases	400	2.55	1,020				400		1,020
Balance							850	2.50	2,122.20
" 28 Sales				300	2.50	750	550		1,372.20
Dec. 1 Purchases	200	2.70	540				200		540
Balance							750	2.55	1,912.20
" 23 Sales				100	2.55	255			
Balance							650	2.55	1,657.20
Total			10,105	Cost of sales		9,707.80			

Note: To avoid the constant bias of 'rounding up' the average unit balance price, some of the 'Sales' figures have been slightly adjusted.

QUESTION 10

Schurig Co. Ltd

(a) Statement of Sources and Applications of Funds for year ended 31 December 19X2

Sources		£000
Arising from operations		1,020
Items not involving movement in funds:		
Depreciation		780
Loss on asset disposal		210
		2,010
* Disposal of Fixed Assets		1,200
Disposal of Investments		2,400
		5,610

Applications -		
* Purchase of fixed assets		(5,100)
Dividends paid		(360)
Increase in stock	(90)	
Increase in debtors	(60)	
Decrease in creditors	(150)	
Increase in short term loans	240	
Increase in working capital		(60)
Increase in liquid funds		90

* Amount received on disposal of assets =	
Opening Plant & Equipment	£000
as at 31 December 19X1	13,200
Add purchases	5,100
	18,300
Less Depreciation and loss	990
	17,310
Balance at 31 December 19X2	16,110
. . Amount received	1,200

(a)   Statement of Sources and Applications of Funds for year ended 31 December 19X3

	£000
Sources	
Arising from operations	1,230
Items not involving movements in funds	
Depreciation	900
	2,130
Disposal of investments	510
	2,640
Applications	
Purchase of fixed assets	(1,200)
Payment of dividends	(360)
Increase in stock	(210)
Increase in debtors	(330)
Increase in creditors	60
Decrease in short-term loans	(30)
	(510)
Increase in liquid funds	570

(£2,580,000 - £2,010,000 = £570,000)

QUESTION 11   GLAZINGS

Statement of Sources and Application of Funds for year ending 31 December 19X2

	£000
Sources	
Operations	180
Add Items not involving movement in funds	
Depreciation	68
Loss on disposal of asset	9.2
	257.2
Disposal of asset	6.8
	264
Issue of debenture	60
	324
Applications	
Acquisition of plant	(460)
Payment of dividend	(16)
Payment of tax	(60)
Increase in stock	(30)
Increase in debtors	(72)
Increase in creditors	48 (54)
Decrease in liquid funds	(266)
(£276,000 - £10,000) =	£266,000

Chapter 7

QUESTION 1   J and I BOWNUS

Points to be raised:

(i)(a)   The balance sheet merely reflects the results of past transactions and, in particular, fixed assets are included at historic cost less amounts written off as depreciation.

(b)   A valuation of the business as a whole would be undertaken by any potential buyer.   This could be by either:

(1)   revaluing all existing assets and by separately attempting to value goodwill. The resulting balance sheet will then show the capital accounts of the partners at the net worth of any offer.

(2)   Attempting a global valuation of the business without reference to any particular assets taken over and assuming that goodwill is the difference between the offer price and the existing net worth.

(ii)   As related on page 90 of the text, an analysis of goodwill is not undertaken.   Nevertheless, this question implicitly requires some general observations on this matter.   The money measurement convention in a case such as this would not allow for the appearance of the relevant assets in the balance sheet.

The assets which the potential purchaser would like to acquire are:

(1)   the artistic skill of the partners;

(2)   the skill and competency of the assistants;

(3)   the reputation and contacts of the firm.

All these factors are not on the balance sheet as they did not come into existence as a result of a transaction requiring an accounting entry.   However, these are the very bases of the business and are commonly recognized as 'goodwill' in any purchase.

Traditionally, goodwill of small businesses has been separately valued as some number of years 'super' profits where the super profits means earnings above the average achieved in the particular trade or industry.   There may be a case here for valuing the total earnings stream as it may be difficult to ascertain what would constitute normal earnings in a business such as this to apply the usual goodwill valuation.

The issues raised here are beyond the scope of this text and students can return to them at more advanced stages of study.

QUESTION 2   DAVID LAWRENCE

Profit and Loss Account for year ended 30 June 19X7

(1) and (2)

	Accrual Basis		Cash Basis	
	£	£	£	£
Rents		6,625		7,125
Less: Rates	1,525		1,780	
Repairs and renewals	267		267	
Insurances	68		68	
Electricity	357	2,217	492	2,607
Net profit for year		4,408		4,518

Notes (1) - Accrual system

	£
Rents: Total receivable	
Properties 1 and 2	2,000
Properties 3 and 4	3,000
Property 5	2,000
	7,000

The conservatism convention would require that uncollected rent on property No. 4 be excluded	375
	6,625

Rates

Cash paid Properties 1 and 2	640
Properties 3 and 4	720
Property 5	420
	1,780
Add Prepaid rates 30 June 19X6	1,080
	2,850
Less Prepaid rates 30 June 19X7	1,335
	1,525

Electricity

Cash paid	492
Add amount unpaid 30.6.19X7	78
	570
Less amount unpaid 30.6.19X6	118
	452
Less amounts collectable	95
	357

(2) Cash basis

Rents received	£
Properties 1 and 2	2,000
Properties 3 and 4	2,625
Property 5	2,500
	7,125

All other figures would simply be the actual cash paid.

QUESTION 3 BOND LTD AND ENLAYE LTD

		(i) Bond Ltd £	(ii) Enlaye Ltd £
Reported Profit		120,000	120,000
Depreciation adjustment	+	6,000	- 6,000
Research and development	+	8,692	- 9,500
Stock adjustment	-	11,000	+ 9,000
		123,692	113,500
Financing - Debenture interest			6,600
		123,692	120,100

Although the choice of financing by debenture is not an alternative 'accounting treatment' in the way that the other items are, the introduction of interest can hinder true comparability. Hence, the amount is added back to ensure proper comparison.

QUESTION 4 GEORGE FROBISHER

Cash and Bank Summary - to 30 June 19X1

	£		£
Capital	5,000	Seeds - Lettuce etc.	150
Herb sales	600	" Sunflower	500
Lettuce etc. sales	1,200	Manure and fertilizer	300
		Van	1,600
		Tractor	2,000
		Herbs	250
		Personal drawings	1,300
		Motor expenses	610
		Balance - Bank	50
		Cash	40
	6,800		6,800
Balance - Bank	50		
Cash	40		

(It can be assumed that all information supplied is correct and that Frobisher is thus holding cash in hand amounting to £40.)

Revised Profit and Loss Account for 6 months to 30 June 19X1

	£	£
Sales		1,800
Less Cost of sales		
Purchase of seeds etc.	1,200	
Less Closing stock	725	475
Surplus		1,325
Less - Motor expenses	610	
Depreciation	350	960
Net profit for period		365

Notes

(1) Stock is calculated as	£
All of sunflower seeds at cost	500
Two thirds of the lettuce seed	100
One half of the herb plants	125
Manure and Fertilizer	0
	725

(2) It may well be considered prudent to disregard the profit from sales of herbs. However, the claim against Frobisher is vague and the matter has obviously not yet been settled.

(3) The decline in value of the tractor and the van can be used as a basis for depreciation but more information would be needed to finally adjust this figure.

(4) The increase in the value of land has not been realized and could thus not be included as profit. If evidence is forthcoming supporting the claim that the value has increased it may well be that this would be useful in securing a loan.

Other factors, apart from those raised in (1) to (4) above, which would need to be examined in any request for a loan are

(a) How far are the figures for projected sales of products supported by evidence?

(b) Does the revised profit figure reflect the seasonal nature of the business?

QUESTION 5   MAINCHANCE COMPUTER DATING

Bank account - Summary to 31 October 19X9

19X9			£	19X9			£
Sept.	1	G. Whiteside Capital	250	Sept.	1	Six months' rent	200
Sept.	1	Loan - Mrs. Whiteside	1,000	Sept.	1	Advertisements	480
Oct.	31	Receipts	2,400	Oct.	31	Advertisements	140
				Oct.	31	Cheques returned unpaid	48
						Computer time	500
						Balance c/d	2,282
			3,650				3,650
19X9							
Oct.	31	Balance b/d	2,282				

Profit and Loss Account for two months to 31 October 19X9

	£	£
Fees earned		2,352
Less expenses		
Rental - Premises	66	
Rental Computer time	500	
Advertisements	620	
Damages claim	75	1,261
		1,091

Balance Sheet as of 31 October 19X9

Mainchance Computer Dating

		£
Assets		
Bank	2,282	
Prepaid rent	134	
	2,416	
Less Claim damages	75	2,341
Less: Creditors amount falling due after more than a year		
Loan - Mrs Whiteside		1,000
		1,341
Capital - G. Whiteside		250
Net profit for period		1,091
		1,341

Notes: (a) Conservation has been applied in as far as income from fees has only been recognized when cash has been received. No promises or future claims for services have been included. The position of the 14 unfulfilled datings has not yet been clarified.

(b) The potential damages claim has been recognized.

(c) Part of the premises has been treated as a normal prepayment.

(d) All advertisements have been treated as an immediate expense although the benefits may still flow in fugure.

QUESTIONS 6 - 8

These questions are included to allow the tutor and student to discuss the concept, use and limitations of standards. It is not expected that students on introductory courses will be required to read further than *Accounting Theory and Practice* and *Basic Accounting Practice*. However, it is hoped that this introduction to the subject will allow students to appreciate that the study of accounting is not confined to mechanistic exercises with 'right answers' and that the adoption of conventions of a simplistic nature eventually can lead to grave problems.

Illustrations of this may be given briefly.

e.g. Adoption of:

cost convention leads to inflation accounting problems;

going concern convention leads to assumptions about decisions not yet made;

money measurement convention leads to omission of vital data;

entity conventions gives rise to difficulties in the recognition of groups who have a legitimate interest in performance of enterprises.

Chapter 8

QUESTIONS 1, 2, 3, 4, 5

These are intended to serve as possible essay or discussion topics. At an introductory level the student can only be expected to offer limited observations and
comment but a more comprehensive treatment can be followed in *Accounting Theory
and Practice* by Glautier and Underdown.

QUESTION 6   G.E. & R. MAIN CO. LTD

Statement of source and application of funds for the year ended 30 September 19X7

	£000s	£000s
Source of Funds		
Profit before tax		32
Adjustment for items not involving the movement of funds:		
Depreciation		22
Loss on sale of fixtures		24
Total generated from operations		78
Funds from other sources		
Proceeds from sale of fixtures 70 - (24 + 15)		31
Issue of new shares 25 + 10		35
Issue of debentures		15
		150
Application of Funds		
Dividends paid	8	
Purchase of property	90	
Purchase of fittings	100	198
Change in Working Capital		(48)
Increase in stocks	37	
Increase in trade debtors	29	
Decrease in trade creditors	(36)	
	18	
Movement in net Liquid Funds		
Decrease in bank balance	(66)	(48)

QUESTION 7 DOMESTICE EQUIPMENT CO. LTD

Statement of source and application of funds for the year ended 31 December 19X7

	£000s	£000s
(a) Source of Funds		
Profit before tax		560
Adjustment for items not involving the movement of funds:		
Depreciation		100
Total generated from operations		660
Application of Funds		
Dividends paid	160	
Purchase of plant and equipment 800 - (600-60)	260	
Purchase of motor vehicles 300 - (200-40)	140	
Taxation paid	170	
		730
Change in Working Capital		(70)
Increase in stocks	140	
Increase in trade debtors	20	
Increase in trade creditors	(30)	
	130	
Movement in Net Liquid Funds		
Decrease in bank balance	(200)	
		(70)

(b) Profitability Ratios

	19X2	19X3
Gross margin ratio	40%	42%
Net profit ratio	20%	23%
Return on capital employed	36%	45%
Activity Ratios		
Stock turnover	5X	4.4X
Debtors' collection period	33 days	30 days
Sales value to NAV	1.8	1.9
Solvency Ratios		
Current ratio	1.5	1.2
Acid test ratio	0.8	0.7
Gearing ratios		
Borrowed finance to Equity	1:10	1:11
Borrowed finance to total funds	1:11	1:12
External claims as percentage of total assets	41%	41%

(c) The flow of funds statement for 19X3 shows that a substantial amount was spent on fixed assets which accounts for the decline in working capital during that year and, in particular, the fall in the balance of cash at the bank. The profitability ratios based on margins appear to be stable but the return on capital employed has increased considerably from 19X2 to 19X3. Students can be expected to offer some explanations for this.

QUESTION 8

The ratio analysis for Bigdeal Stores Ltd is shown below as falling into two sections. The first, and largest, is based on the figures as given in the accounting results and the second is based on market information taken in conjunction with the accounting figures.

Section 1 - Accounting Ratios

(a) Profitability Ratios   19X2   19X3

Gross margin ratio   Not available

(It is important to note that the use of the term 'Trading Income' or 'Trading Profit' in published accounts is NOT the same as the accounting use of the term meaning sales less cost of sales.)

Net Profit Ratio $\left(\dfrac{13,814}{178,392}\right) \times 100 = 7.7\%$ $\left(\dfrac{11,553}{191,423}\right) \times 100 = 6\%$

Return on capital employed $\dfrac{13,814}{67,428} \times 100 = 20.4\%$ $\dfrac{11,553}{90,814} \times 100 = 12.7\%$

(b) Activity Ratios

Stock turnover   6   5

Debtors' collection period   Insufficient information as to ratio of credit sales to cash sales

Sales value to NAV   2.6   2.1

(c) Solvency Ratios

Current ratio   1.5   1.1

Acid test ratio   .4   .07

(d) Gearing Ratios

Borrowed finance to equity   1:3.5   1:3.5

Borrowed finance to total funds 1:4.5   1:4.5

Claims as percentage of total assets   43%   43%

Section 2 Ratios using market and accounting data

	19X2	19X3

(a) Earnings per share $\dfrac{6,604}{20,000} = 33p$ $\dfrac{3,386}{20,000} = 16.9p$

Dividend yield $10\% \times \dfrac{20,000}{84,000} = 2.4\%$ $12.5\% \times \dfrac{20,000}{100,000} = 2.5\%$

Dividend cover $\dfrac{6,604}{2,000} = 3.3$ $\dfrac{3,386}{2,500} = 1.4$

Earnings yield $2.4\% \times 3.3 = 7.92\%$ $2.5\% \times 1.4 = 3.5\%$

Price earning ratios $\dfrac{4.20}{33p} = 13$ $\dfrac{5.00}{16.9} = 29$

Comments:

Students will be expected to recognize the decline in profitability and to note the dangerous liquidity levels.

Surprise may be experience at the market price in 19X3 in the light of the foregoing.

Part 2   Accounting for Planning and Control
Chapter 9

QUESTION 1

		Direct/Indirect Costs	Fixed/Variable Costs
1	Factory heating	Indirect	Fixed
2	Advertising	Indirect	Fixed
3	Operator's wages	Direct	Variable
4	Depreciation of machinery	Indirect	Fixed
5	Machinery repairs	Indirect	Variable
6	Personnel department	Indirect	Fixed
7	Consumable tools used in production	Direct	Variable
8	Raw materials used in production	Direct	Variable
9	Packing	Direct	Variable
10	Salesmen's salaries	Indirect	Fixed
11	Production manager's salary	Indirect	Fixed
12	Factory rent	Indirect	Fixed
13	Power	Indirect	Variable
14	Machinery and equipment insurance	Indirect	Fixed
15	Carriage inwards	Direct	Variable
16	Storekeeper's salary	Indirect	Fixed

Notes

(1) It should be stressed that costs are defined as fixed only in relation to planned output. As output increases, fixed costs tend to vary in a 'stepped' fashion.

(2) Mixed costs should be classified into fixed and variable components.

(3) Some costs shown as variables may sometimes be treated as fixed. Thus direct labour costs, which are usually treated as variable may, in effect, become fixed if Government regulations make it impossible for management to lay-off employees at will.

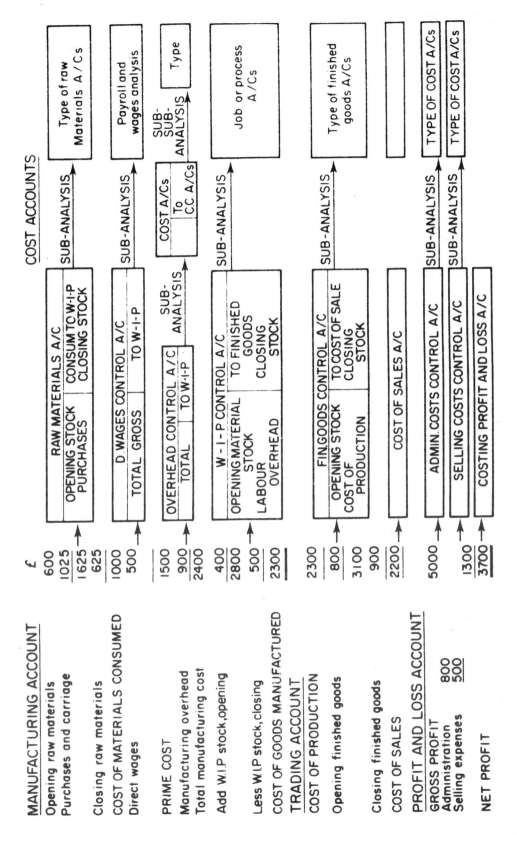

QUESTION 3 PROFIT REPORTING

Imperial Manufacturing Company Statements of Cost of Goods Sold for the years ended 31 December

	19X1 £	19X2 £
Direct materials		
Raw materials stock 1 January	10,000	12,000
Raw materials purchases	40,000	43,000
	50,000	55,000
Raw materials stock 31 December	12,000	15,000
	38,000	40,000
Direct labour	30,000	35,000
Factory overhead	19,000	25,000
Manufacturing cost incurred in 19X1 and 19X2	87,000	100,000
Add: Work-in-progress stock 1 January	20,000	22,000
	107,000	122,000
Less: Work-in-progress stock 31 December	22,000	24,000
Cost of goods manufactured	85,000	98,000
Add: Finished goods stock 1 January	30,000	25,000
	115,000	123,000
Less: Finished goods stock 31 December	25,000	28,000
Cost of goods sold	90,000	95,000

QUESTION 4 PROFIT REPORTING

Alpine Manufacturing Company Statement of Cost of Goods Sold during the year ended 31 December 19X1

	£	£
Direct materials:		
Raw materials stock 1 January 19X1	60,000	
Raw materials purchases	100,000	
	160,000	
Raw materials stock 31 December 19X1	45,000	
Raw materials used		115,000
Direct labour		85,000

Factory overheads:

Supplies	15,000	
Supervision	20,000	
Inspection	10,000	
Other indirect labour	30,000	
Depreciation	15,000	
Heat, light and power	10,000	
Insurance	6,000	
Factory overhead costs for the year		106,000
Manufacturing costs incurred		306,000
Add: Work-in-progress stock 1 January 19X1		20,000
		326,000
Less: Work-in-Progress stock 31 December 19X1		25,000
Cost of goods manufactured		301,000
Add: Finished goods stock 1 January 19X1		95,000
		396,000
Less: Finished goods stock 31 December 19X1		100,000
Cost of goods sold		296,000

Alpine Manufacturing Company Profit Statement for the year ended 31 December 19X1

	£	£
Sales		500,000
		296,000
Gross profit		204,000
Selling and administrative expenses:		
Sales salaries	12,000	
Administrative salaries	20,000	
Stationery, supplies and postages	1,000	
Depreciation	11,000	
		44,000
Net profit		160,000

QUESTION 5 CALCULATION OF OVERHEAD RATES

Overhead Costs	Basis	Drilling	Milling	Assembly	Maintenance	Canteen	Total
		£	£	£	£	£	£
Indirect materials	Direct	50,000	15,000	80,000	60,000	85,000	290,000
Indirect labour	Direct	40,000	20,000	100,000	80,000	40,000	280,000
Heat and light	Direct	10,000	8,000	15,000	20,000	15,000	68,000
Factory rent	Floor space	25,000	20,000	35,000	10,000	10,000	100,000
Supervisory salaries	Employees	55,000	35,000	75,000	20,000	15,000	200,000
		180,000	98,000	305,000	190,000	165,000	938,000
Apportionment							
Maintenance	Manhours	57,000	38,000	95,000	(190,000)		
Canteen	Employees	55,000	35,000	75,000	-	(165,000)	
		292,000	171,000	475,000	-	-	938,000
Overhead Rate							
Machine hours		60,000	40,000	100,000			
Machine hour rate		£4.87	£4.27	£4.74			

QUESTION 6   ABSORPTION OF OVERHEAD COSTS TO PRODUCTS

(1) Computation of predetermined overhead rates

		Dept. A	Dept. B
(a)	Direct labour cost rate	£450,000	£415,000
		£200,000	£ 50,000
		= 225% of	= 830% of
		direct labour	direct labour
		costs	costs
(b)	Direct labour hour rate	£450,000	£415,000
		150,000 hrs	25,000 hrs
		= £3.00 per	= £16,60 per
		direct labour	direct labour
		hour	hour
(c)	Machine hour rate	£450,000	£450,000
		100,000 hrs	415,000 hrs
		= £4.50 per	= £1.00 per
		machine hour	machine hour

(2) The direct labour cost method is relatively easy to use, since the information needed to calculate the overhead rate is readily available. This method, however, may be criticized for two reasons. First, many overhead cost items are fixed, and therefore are a function of time rather than labour cost. Second, this method may lead to an inaccurate distribution of factory overhead costs, particularly when numerous operators paid on the basis of different hourly rates of pay are employed in the same department.

The direct labour hour method partly overcomes the disadvantages of the direct labour cost method, and would be suitable for use as regards Dept. A which is labour intensive.

The machine hour rate method may be the most accurate method of applying overhead costs to jobs in Dept. B, which is machine intensive, and where there appears to be a relationship between overhead costs incurred and the number of machine hours.

(3) Computation of job order costs

	Job 101 £	Job 102 £	Job 103 £
Direct materials	1,000	800	1,500
Direct labour	2,500	2,800	3,600
Overhead costs applied:			
Dept. A - direct labour hour rate	4,800	6,000	8,400
Dept. B - machine hour rate	2,000	2,500	3,000
	10,300	12,100	16,500

105

QUESTION 7 CAPACITY LEVELS FOR COMPUTING FACTORY OVERHEAD RATES

(1) Calculation of Direct Labour Hour Rate

	Capacity Level		
	Practical	Expected	Normal
Activity level as a percentage of theoretical capacity	90%	75%	80%
Activity level in units	450,000	375,000	400,000
Activity level in direct labour hours	90,000	75,000	80,000
Fixed factory overhead costs	£150,000	£150,000	£150,000
Variable factory overhead costs (£0.3 per unit)	135,000	112,000	120,000
Total factory overhead costs	285,000	262,500	270,000
Direct labour hour rate	£3.17	£3.51	£3.37

(2) Reference should be made to the discussion of normal capacity in *Accounting Theory and Practice*. Normal capacity is the most appropriate capacity level to use for determining overhead rates because it reflects the firm's long-run ability to product and to sell.

QUESTION 8 INTRODUCTION TO COST ACCUMULATION

(1)

Job 101	Material £	Labour £	Overheads £	Total £	Status I F D
Balance Jan 1	10,000	3,000	2,000	15,000	
Added during Jan	12,000	41,000	30,000	83,000	
Total Jan 31	22,000	44,000	32,000	98,000	X

Job 101	Material £	Labour £	Overheads £	Total £	Status I F D
Balance Jan 1	15,000	8,000	2,000	25,000	
Added during Jan	6,000	25,000	18,000	49,000	
Total Jan 31	21,000	33,000	20,000	74,000	X

Job 103	Material £	Labour £	Overheads £	Total £	Status I F D
Balance Jan 1	2,000	1,000	1,000	4,000	
Added during Jan	14,000	8,000	6,000	28,000	
Total Jan 31	16,000	9,000	7,000	32,000	X

(2) Factory Overhead account

	£		£
Materials	8,000	Job 101	30,000
Labour	10,000	Job 102	18,000
Other expenses	40,000	Job 103	6,000
		Balance c/d	4,000
	58,000		58,000
Balance b/d	4,000		

(3) The Factory Overhead account shows that a higher overhead cost has been incurred than has been recovered. The balance of £4,000 arises, therefore, because of an 'under-application' of overheads to the three jobs. The reasons why overheads have been under-applied may have been due to:

(a) estimating errors made in the course of calculating the predetermined overhead rate:

(b) higher actual overhead costs being incurred than those which were anticipated;

(c) output may have been smaller than was planned, with the result that fixed costs were not entirely recovered;

(d) seasonal factors may account for the discrepancy between planned and actual overhead costs.

QUESTION 9   PREPARING 'T' ACCOUNTS FOR A JOB ORDER SYSTEM

(1)(a) Control Accounts

Raw Materials account

Bal.	5,000	20,000	(2)	
(1)	25,000	10,000	Bal.	
	20,000	30,000		
Bal.	10,000			

Work-in-Progress account

Bal.	10,000	59,800	(7)	
(2)	20,000			
(3)	22,000			
(6)	23,100	15,300	Bal.	
	75,100	75,100		
Bal.	15,300			

Finished Goods account

Bal.	20,000	66,000	(8)	
(7)	62,800	16,800	Bal.	
	82,000	82,800		
Bal.	16,800			

(b) Subsidiary Ledgers

Materials Ledger
Material X account

	£	£		
Bal.	2,000	5,000	(2)	
(1)	10,000	7,000	Bal.	
	12,000	12,000		
Bal.	7,000			

Job Ledger
Job 100 account

	£	£	
Bal.	7,000	7,000	(7)
	Job 101	account	
	£	£	
Bal.	3,000	3,000	(7)

Finished Goods Ledger
Product A-account

	£	£	
Bal.	10,000	35,000	(8)
	32,000	7,000	Bal.
	42,000	42,000	
Bal.	7,000		

Material Y account

£		£	
Bal.	2,000	11,000	(2)
(1)	10,000	1,000	Bal.
	12,000	12,000	
Bal.	1,000		

Job 102 account

£		£	
(2)	10,000	22,000	(7)
(3)	6,000		
(6)	6,000		
	22,000	22,000	

Product B account

£		£	
Bal.	8,000	30,000	(8)
(7)	30,800	8,800	Bal.
	38,800	38,800	
Bal.	8,800		

Job 103 account

£		£	
(2)	8,000	27,800	(7)
(3)	9,000		
(6)	10,800		
	27,800	27,800	

Material Z account

£		£	
Bal.	1,000	4,000	(2)
(1)	5,000	2,000	Bal.
	6,000	6,000	
Bal.	2,000		

Job 104 account

£		£	
(2)	2,000		
(3)	7,000		
(6)	6,300	15,300	Bal.
	15,300	15,300	
Bal.	15,300		

Product C account

£		£	
Bal.	2,000	1,000	(8)
		1,000	Bal.
	2,000	2,000	
Bal.	1,000		

(c)

Factory Overheads account

£		£	
(2)	3,000	23,100	(6)
(3)	8,000	900	Bal.
(4)	10,000		
(5)	3,000		
	24,000	24,000	
Bal.	900		

(2) Agreement of Control and Subsidiary Accounts

Control Accounts		Subsidiary Ledgers	
Raw materials	10,000	Material X	7,000
		Material Y	1,000
		Material Z	2,000
Work-in-progress	15,300	Job No. 104	15,300
Finished goods	16,800	Product A	7,000
		Product B	8,800
		Product C	1,000

QUESTION 10 PREPARING A PRODUCTION COST REPORT

Production Cost Report for the month ending 31 January 19X1

Department B

	Physical flow	Equivalent Units Materials	Equivalent Units Conversion costs
Quantities			
Work-in-progress, opening stock	200		
Units transferred in	6,400		
Total units to be accounted for	6,600		
Units transferred out	6,300	6,300	6,300
Work-in-progress, closing stock	300	(2/3) 200	(1/3) 100
	6,600	6,500	6,400

Costs	Total	Materials	Conversion	Transferred in
	£	£	£	£
Work-in-progress, opening stock	470	50	70	350
Current costs of period	25,530	3,200	11,130	11,200
Total costs to be accounted for	26,000	3,250	11,200	11,550
divide by equivalent units		6,500	6,400	6,600
	4.00	0.50	1.75	1.75

Apportionment of costs	Equivalent Units	Unit Cost	Total Cost
		£	£
Costs transferred out	6,300	4.00	25,200
Work-in-progress, closing stock			
Transferred in costs	300	1.75	525
Materials	200	0.50	100
Conversion	100	1.75	175
Total in progress			800
Total costs accounted for			26,000

QUESTION 11 PROCESS UNIT COSTS AND WORK IN PROGRESS

(a) Incredible Gadget Corporation: Computation of Unit Costs for the month
ended 31 May 19X1

Machining Dept.

Materials	75,000	75,000	120,000	1.60
Labour	75,000	65,000	87,100	1.34
Overheads	75,000	65,000	39,000	0.60
Transferred to Assembly and Finishing Dept.			246,100	3.54
Closing stock of work-in-progress	60,000	60,000	212,400	
			33,700	

Assembly and Finishing Dept., materials:

Cost of materials added	60,000	59,500	41,650	0.70
Cost of materials spoiled	1,000	500	350	0.70
Transferred to Finished Goods			41,300	
Closing stock of material in process	50,000	50,000	35,000	0.70
			6,300	

Labour:

Cost of labour	60,000	56,500	101,700	1.80
Cost of labour in spoiled units	1,000	500	900	1.80
			100,800	
Transferred to Finished Goods	50,000	50,000	90,000	1.80
Closing stock of labour in process			10,800	

Overheads:

Cost of overheads	60,000	56,000	56,810	
Spoiled units:				
Machining Dept. costs			3,540	
Assembly and Finishing Dept. costs				
Materials			350	
Labour			900	
	60,000	56,000	61,600	1.10
Transferred to Finished Goods	50,000	50,000	55,000	1.10
Closing stock of overheads in progress			6,600	

110

Summary of Unit Costs for May:

Machining Dept.:		
Materials	1.60	
Labour	1.34	
Overheads	0.60	3.54
Assembly and Finishing Dept.:		
Materials	0.70	
Labour	1.80	
Overheads	1.10	3.60
Total		7.14

(b) Summary of Work-in-Progress at 31 May 19X1

	Percent complete	Amount £
Machining Dept. 15,000 units:		
Materials	100	24,000
Labour	33 1/3	6,700
Overheads	33 1/3	3,000
		33,700
Assembly and Finishing Dept.:		
Transferred costs from Machining Dept.	100	31,860
Materials	100	6,300
Labour	66 2/3	10,800
Overheads	66 2/3	6,600
		55,560
Total Work-in-Progress 31 May 19X1		89,260

QUESTION 12 THE TREATMENT OF WASTE IN PROCESS ACCOUNTS

The Northern Refining Company Ltd.

	Tons	£	Crushing Process account	Tons	£	Cost per ton
Raw materials	1,500	15,000	Sale of bags		350	
Direct materials added		1,100	Normal waste	150		
Wages		2,200	Output transferred out	1,250	17,500	14
Power		650				
Sundry expenses		300	Abnormal waste	100	1,400	
	1,500	19,250		1,500	19,250	

Refining Process account

	Units	£		Units	£	
Output transferred in	1,250	17,500	Normal waste	250	1,000	
Direct materials added		1,780	Output transferred out	1,000	20,000	20
Wages		980				
Power		460				
Sundry expenses		280				
		21,000		1,250	21,000	

Finishing Process account

	Units	£		Units	£	
Output transferred in	1,000	20,000	Normal waste	100	200	
Direct materials added		900	Balance carried down	900	23,400	26
Wages		2,190				
Power		360				
Sundry expenses		150				
	1,000	23,600		1,000	23,600	
Balance brought down	900	23,724	Finished product transferred to cost of sales	900	24,300	27
Fitting into drums		900				
	900	24,624		900	24,300	

QUESTION 13   PROCESS ACCOUNTS

Process 1 account

Input Units		£	Output Units		£
10,000	Basic raw material	6,000	9,200	@ £2.50 to Process 2	23,000
	Direct material added	8,500	(200)	Abnormal gain account @ £2.50 p.u.	(500)
	Direct wages	4,000			
	Direct expenses	1,200			
	Production overhead: £16,500/£22,000 = 75% D.W.	3,000			
		22,700			
	Credit Normal loss				
(1,000)	10% Input @ £0.20 p.u.	(200)			
9,000		£22,500	9,000		£22,500

Process 2 account

Input Units			Output Units		
9,200	From Process 1	23,000	8,700	@ £5.0 to Process 3	43,500
	Direct material added	9,500	40	Abnormal loss account @ £5.00 p.u.	200
	Direct wages	6,000			
	Direct expenses	930			
	Production overhead:				
	75% Direct wages	4,500			
		43,930			
	Credit Normal loss				
(460)	5% Input @ £0.50 p.u.	(230)			
8,740		£43,700	8,740		£43,700

Process 3 account

Input Units			Output Units		
8,700	From Process 2	43,500	7,900	@ £9.00 to Finished Stock	71,100
	Direct material added	5,500	(70)	Abnormal gain account @ £9.0 p.u.	(630)
	Direct wages	12,000			
	Direct expenses	1,340			
	Production overhead:				
	75% Direct wages	9,000			
		71,340			
	Credit Normal loss				
(870)	10% Input @ £1.00	(870)			
7,830		£70,470	7,830		£70,470

Abnormal loss account

Apl. 30	Transfer: Process 2 40 units @ £5 p.u.	200	Apl. 30	Scrap recovery: 40 units @ £0.5	20
				Balance c/f	180
		200			200
May 1	Balance b/f	180			

Apl. 30	Shortage on scrap recovery:		Apl. 30	Transfer: Process 1	
	Pr. 1 200 units @ £0.20 p.u.	.40		200 units @ £2.50	500
	Pr. 3 70 units @ £1.00 p.u.	.70		Transfer: Process 3	
	Balance c/f	1,020		70 units @ £9.00	630
		1,130			1,130
			May 1	Balance b/f	1,020

(<u>Note</u>: The above figures may be checked as follows:

	£	£
Total cost		71,470
Scrap recovery:		
Process 1 800 × £0.20	160	
2 500 × £0.50	250	
3 800 × £1.00	800	(1,210)
		£70,260
Represented by:		
Finished stock		71,100
Abnormal loss account		180
Abnormal gain account		(1,020)
		£70,260

QUESTION 14   JOINT PRODUCTS

Statement showing the total cost and the cost per kilo of the joint products A, B and C

	Total £	A £	B £	C £
Cost up to split-off point				
Direct material	3,250			
Direct labour	1,704			
Manufacturing overheads	1,934			
Total costs up to split-off point	6,888			
Appointed to joint products in proportion to sales value of finished products	6,888	2,009	2,583	2,296
Cost after split-off point				
Direct material	2,690	600	1,090	1,000
Direct labour	1,910	420	780	710
Manufacturing overheads	1,078	233	227	618
	£12,566	£3,262	£4,680	£4,624
Production in kilos		700	600	400
Cost per kilo		£4.66	£7.80	£11.56

Each of the products is of substantial value therefore treat them as joint products. The proportions of sales value of the three products differ considerably from the proportions of their weights. Applying the principle that the greater the sales value of a product, the greater is the cost which can be borne by that product, the costs at point of split-off are divided in proportion to sales value.

QUESTION 15   JOINT PRODUCTS AND BY-PRODUCTS

The net sales value of Product C is negligible compared with that of A and B, the related values for each 100 kilos of input into process 2 being:

A 40 kilos at £3 per 100 kilos	£1.20	
B 30 kilos at £4 per 100 kilos	£1.20	
C 20 kilos at 20 pence per 100 kilos	£0.04	
Waste 10 kilos	no value	
100		

The net return is:

	Selling price £	Further costs £	Net return £
A 40 kilos	1.20	-	1.20
B 30 kilos	1.20	0.30	0.90
C 20 kilos	0.04	0.01	0.03
Waste 10 kilos	-	-	-

It is evident from the above that product B should be treated as a by-product, the net sales value thereof going to reduce the total cost at the end of process 2.

The cost at this point should be apportioned to products A and B on some equitable basis. It seems apparent that the basis in this case is to charge product A with 4/7 ths and B with 3/7 ths of the cost at the point of split-off, for both weight of products and net return for the products are in these proportions.

A skeleton cost statement would appear as follows:

	Weight kilos	Cost £
Process 1		
Input	100	
Charges	-	
Increase in weight	5	—
	105	—
Process 2		
Input	105	
Charges	-	
Less: Waste (no value)	10.5	
	94.5	
Less: Net sales value of product C	21.0	
	73.5	

Apportioned to joint products
on basis of weight:

A	42.0
B	31.5
	73.5

QUESTION 16   SEPARATE COST AND FINANCIAL ACCOUNTING SYSTEM

(a)

Raw materials control account

			£					£
Mar	1	To Balance b/f	50,836	May	31	By transfer to W.I.P. control		16,290
May	31	To Purchases	22,422	May	31	By returns		836
				May	31	By raw material losses		1,236
				May	31	By balance c/f		54,896
			73,258					73,258
June	1	To balance b/f	54,896					

Work-in-progress control account

Mar	1	Balance b/f	12,745	May	31	By transfer to finished stock control	36,834
May	31	To Factory overhead	11,786	May	31	By rejects	1,764
May	31	To Direct wages	8,370	May	31	By balance c/f	10,593
May	31	To Raw materials	16,290				
			49,191				49,191
June	1	To Balance b/f	10,593				

Finished stock control account

Mar	1	To Balance b/f	25,980	May	31	By transfer to cost of sales	41,389
May	31	To transfer from W.I.P. control	36,834	May	31	By balance c/f	24,281
May	31	To Sales returns	2,856				
			65,670				65,670
June	1	Balance b/f	24,281				

116

Cost ledger control account

		£				£
May 31	To Fin. stock control (cost of sales)	41,389	May 1	By balance b/f		89,561
May 31	To Raw mat. control (returns)	836	May 31	By W.I.P. control (Fact. overhead)		11,786
May 31	To Raw mat. control (losses)	1,236	May 31	By raw mat. control (purchases)		22,422
May 31	To W.I.P. control (rejects)	1,764	May 31	By W.I.P. control (direct wages)		8,370
May 31	To Balance c/f	89,770	May 31	By Fin. stock control (returns)		2,856
		134,995				134,995
			June 1	By Balance b/f		89,770

(b) Schedule of balances as at 1 June

	Dr	Cr
	£	£
Raw materials control account	54,896	
Work-in-progress control account	10,593	
Finished stock control account	24,281	
Cost ledger control account		89,770
	89,770	89,770

QUESTION 17   SEPARATE COST AND FINANCIAL ACCOUNTING SYSTEM

Cost ledger (for year ended 31 October 19X4)

(a)

Raw materials control account

	£	£		£
Balance b/f		230,244	Issues to W.I.P. account	942,010
			Balance c/f	241,612
Purchases	972,102			
Returns	18,724	953,378		
		1,183,622		1,183,622
Balance b/f		241,612		

(b)   Work-in-progress ledger control account

	£			
Balance b/f		130,546	Transfer to Fin. goods account	1,523,918
R.M. issues		942,010	Balance c/f	137,226
Direct wages	£			
Paid	256,483			
Accrued	23,797	280,280		
Production overhead 110% direct wages		308,308		
		1,661,144		1,661,144
Balance b.f		137,226		

(c)   Finished goods ledger control account

	£		£
Balance b/f	153,148	Transfer to cost of sales account	1,530,281
Transfer from W.I.P. account	1,523,918	Balance c/f	146,785
	1,677,066		1,677,066
Balance b/f	146,785		

(d)   Cost of sales account

	£		£
Finished goods account:		Transfer to Profit and Loss Account	1,803,384
Factory cost	1,530,281		
Administration:			
Salaries	68,724		
Expenses	92,461		
Sales:			
Salaries	24,216		
Expenses	42,586		
Distribution:			
Wages	10,249		
Expenses	34,867		
	1,803,384		1,803,384

(e)   Profit and Loss Account

	£		£
Cost of sales account	1,803,384	Sales	2,124,816
Unabsorbed overhead	34,587	returns	25,921
	1,837,971		
Net profit	260,924		
	2,098,895		2,098,895

QUESTION 18 INTEGRATED COST AND FINANCIAL ACCOUNTING

(All figures in £000s)

Raw material stock account

19X1			£	19X1			£
May	1	Balance b/f	138	May 31		Creditors (returns)	4
	31	Creditors (purchases)	92		31	Transfer to W.I.P.	80
	31	W.I.P. (returns)	2		31	Transfer to Production overhead	10
					31	Balance c/f	138
			232				232
June	1	Balance b/f	138				

Work-in-progress account

May	1	Balance b/f	34	May 31	Raw material (returns)	2
	31	Direct wages	42	31	Abnormal loss	5
	31	Raw materials	80	31	Finished goods	215
	31	Production overhead	105	31	Balance c/f	39
			261			261
June	1	Balance b/f	39			

Finished goods stock account

May	1	Balance b/f	62	May 31	Cost of sales	210
	31	W.I.P.	215	31	Balance c/f	67
			277			277
June	1	Balance b/f	67			

Debtors account

May	1	Balance b/f	200	May 31	Cash	330
	31	Sales	320	31	Discount allowed	11
				31	Balance c/f	179
			520			520
June	1	Balance b/f	179			

Creditors account

May 31	Raw material stock (returns)	4	May 1	Balance b/f	140
31	Cash	101	31	Raw material stock (purchases)	92
31	Discount received	3			
31	Balance c/f	124			
		232			232
			June 1	Balance b/f	124

Expense creditors account

19X1		£	19X1		£
May 31	Cash	140	May 1	Balance b/f	58
31	Balance c/f	85	31	Production overhead	88
			31	Selling & distribution costs	42
			31	Administration costs	37
		225			225
			June 1	Balance b/f	85

Wages account

May 31	Cash	34	May 1	Balance b/f	11
31	P.A.Y.E. deducted	16	31	W.I.P.	42
31	Balance c/f	3			
		53			53
			June 1	Balance b/f	3

P.A.Y.E. tax account

May 31	Balance c/f	61	May 1	Balance b/f	45
			31	Wages	16
		61			61
			June 1	Balance b/f	61

Cash at bank account

May 1	Balance b/f	40	May 31	Creditors	101
31	Debtors	330	31	Expenses creditors	140
			31	Wages	34
			31	Balance c/f	95
		370			370
June 1	Balance b/f	95			

Freehold buildings account

May	1	Balance b.f	360	May 31	Balance c/f	360
June	1	Balance b/f	360			

Plant and machinery account

May	1	Balance of cost b/f	240	May	1	Depreciation to date b/f	60
	31	Balance c/f	62		31	Depreciation for month	
						(Profit and Loss a/c)	2
					31	Balance c/f	240
			302				302
June	1	Balance of cost b/f	240	June	1	Depreciation to date b/f	62

Share capital account

May	31	Balance c/f	600	May	1	Balance b/f	600
				June	1	Balance b/f	600

General reserve account

May	31	Balance c/f	120	May	1	Balance b/f	120
				June	1	Balance b/f	120

Profit and Loss account

May	31	Balance c/f	56	May	1	Balance b/f	40
					31	Profit for month	16
			56				56
				June	1	Balance b/f	56

Sales account

May	31	Profit and loss	320	May 31	Sundries (debtors)	320

Production overhead account

May	31	Expense creditors	88	May 31	W.I.P. account	105
	31	Raw material stock (Prod. maint.)	10			
	31	Balance (overabsorption) c/f	7			
			105				105
				June 1	Balance b/f	7

Selling and distribution costs account

May	31	Expense creditors	42	May 31	Profit and loss account	42

Administration cost account

May	31	Expense creditors	37	May 31	Profit and loss account	37

Abnormal loss account

May	31	W.I.P. account	5	May 31	Profit and loss account	5

Cost of sales account

May	31	Finished goods account	210	May 31	Profit and loss account	210

Discounts account

May	31	Allowed (debtors)	11	May 31	Received (creditors)	3
				31	Profit and loss account	8
			11			11

(b) Profit and loss account for May 19X1

	£		£
Cost of sales	210	Sales	320
Discounts	8		
Depreciation - Plant and machinery	2		
Selling and distribution costs	42		
Administration costs	37		
Abnormal loss	5		
	304		
Balance of profit to cost ledger	16		
Profit and loss account	320		320

Notes. (i) The balance of production overhead over-absorbed has been carried forward
          on the assumption that it would be written off at the end of the year.
     (ii) The abnormal loss has been written off.

Comment Having completed the accounts, students should take out a brief trial balance
(for their own information) to prove their entries.

	Dr £	Cr £
Raw material stock	138	
Work-in-progress	39	
Finished goods stock	67	
Debtors	179	
Creditors		124
Expense creditors		85
Wages accrued		3
P.A.Y.E. Tax		61
Bank	95	
Freehold buildings	360	
Plant and machinery at cost	240	
Plant and machinery depreciation		62
Issued share capital		600
General reserve		120
Profit and loss account		56
Production overhead (over-absorption)		7
	£1,118	£1,118

Chapter 10

QUESTION 1 TRILPORT
Accounting Rate of Return

Year	1	2	3
	£	£	£
Profit	11,000	36,300	65,800
Depreciation	30,000	30,000	30,000
Loss	19,000	Profit 6,300	Profit 35,800

Capital employed	£	£	£
Start of year	100,000	70,000	40,000
End of year	70,000	40,000	10,000
Average for year	85,000	55,000	25,000

$$\text{Average Capital Employed for whole period} = \frac{85,000 + 55,000 + 25,000}{3} = £55,000$$

$$\text{Average profit} = \frac{-19,000 + 6,300 + 35,800}{3} = £7,700$$

$$\text{Accounting rate of return} = \frac{7,700}{55,000} \times 100 = \underline{\underline{14\%}}$$

QUESTION 2 SAMATAN LTD

End of Period	Net Cash Inflow	PV factor 12%	Present Value
	£		£
1	4,000	0.8929	3,572
2	5,500	0.7972	4,385
3	7,000	0.7118	4,983
4	7,000	0.6355	4,448
5	5,500	0.5674	3,121
			20,509
Less Cash outlay at t = 0			- 20,000
Net Present Value			+ 509

Project is acceptable at 12% test rate.

QUESTION 3 LOCMINE LTD
NPV Calculations

Cash inflows £000

	Project					PV factor	Present values				
	A	B	C	D	E	15%	A	B	C	D	E
Year 1	10	15	–	5.5	8	0.8696	8,696	13,044	–	4,783	6,957
" 2	10	15	11	5.5	8	0.7561	7,561	11,341	8,317	4,159	6,049
" 3	10	5	12	5.5	5	0.6575	6,575	3,287	7,890	3,616	3,287
" 4	10	–	15	5.5	5	0.5717	5,717	–	8,575	3,144	2,858
" 5	10	–	2	1.8	3	0.4972	4,972	–	994	895	1,492
" 6	1.5	1	2	1.8	3	0.4323	648	432	865	778	1,297
							34,169	28,104	26,641	17,375	21,940

Less Outlays time 0 –   30,000 30,000 30,000 25,000 25,000

time 1 × 0.8696   8,696

Net Present Values   +4,169 -1,896 -12,055 -7,625 -3,060

From this it can be seen that only Project A would be acceptable using the NPV rule at 15% test rate.

QUESTION 4 LOCMINE LTD
Internal Rates of Return on Projects
A = 20.5%

B = 11%

C = 1.6%

D = 1%

E = 9.4%

QUESTION 5 GORRON LTD
(i) Payback of storage cupboard project

The fixed element of the overhead is not required in the calculations.

Net Cash Flows

	Sales	Less Variable Expense	= N.C.F.
	£	£	£
Year 1	10,000	2,000	8,000
" 2	12,500	2,500	10,000
" 3	13,750	2,750	11,000
" 4	13,750	2,750	11,000
" 5	18,750	3,750	15,000
" 6	18,750	3,750	15,000

Payback = 3 years 2 months (approx.)

(ii) Net Present Value

Net Cash Flow	PV factor	Present Value
£	15%	£
Year 1	8,000	0.8696	6,957
" 2	10,000	0.7561	7,561
" 3	11,000	0.6575	7,232
" 4	11,000	0.5718	6,290
" 5	15,000	0.4972	7,458
" 6	15,000	0.4323	6,484
			41,982
Less Initial outlay			36,000
Net present value of project			+ 5,982

(iii) Internal Rate of Return = 20% approx.

(iv) Accounting Rate of Return

Year	1	2	3	4	5	6
	£	£	£	£	£	£
Profits	400	2,000	2,800	2,800	6,000	6,000
Opening capital	36,000	30,000	24,000	18,000	12,000	6,000
Closing capital	30,000	24,000	18,000	12,000	6,000	- 0 -
Average	33,000	27,000	21,000	15,000	9,000	3,000

Overall average capital employed = £18,000

Average Profits = $\dfrac{20,000}{6}$ = £3,333

Accounting Rate of Return = $\dfrac{3,333}{£8,000}$ × 100 = 18.5%

(v) Present Value Payback (based on cost of capital of 15%)

		£	£ cumulative
Present Value of Cash Flows	Year 1	6,957	6,957
	2	7,561	14,518
	3	7,232	21,750
	4	6,290	28,040
	5	7,458	35,498
	6	6,484	41,982

Payback by Present Value = 5 yrs 1 months approx.

126

QUESTION 6   CONTREST LTD

Cost of equity capital $= \dfrac{36}{2.25} \times 100 = 16\%$

Cost of debentures $= 12\% \times \dfrac{100}{80} = 15\%$

Weighted average cost of capital =

	Market Value £	
Equity 400,000 × £2.25	900,000 × 16& =	144,000
Debentures 80,000	80,000 × (15% ÷ 2)=	6,000
	980,000	150,000

$$\dfrac{150,000}{980,000} \times 100 = 15.3\%$$

QUESTION 7

Present Value of outcomes

Three Million Pound Outlay

Probability	PV of Cash flows £	Expected Present Values £
0.3	5,252,190	1,575,657
0.5	3,725,800	1,862,900
0.2	614,460	122,892
1.0		3,561,449
	Less Outlay	3,000,000
	Expected Net Present Value	£ 561,449

Two Million Pound Outlay

Probability	PV of Cash flows £	Expected Present Values £
0.4	3,389,290	1,355,716
0.4	2,446,880	978,752
0.2	1,228,920	245,784
		2,580,252
	Less Outlay	2,000,000
	Expected Net Present Value	£ 580,252

It can be seen that in expected value terms there is an advantage of approximately £19,000 in adopting the £2m outlay.

Chapter 11

QUESTION 1   PROFIT PERFORMANCE

(i)   Net profit to earn 15% return (in £000s)

$$1500 \times \frac{15}{100} = £225.$$

Operating profit required:

Net profit	£225
Add tax (50%)	112.5
Profit before tax	337.5
Interest	40.0
Operating profit	377.5

$$\frac{\text{Operating profit}}{\text{Total assets}} \times 100 = \frac{377.5}{2,000} \times 100 = \underline{18.9\%}$$

(ii) $\dfrac{\text{Operating profit}}{\text{Sales}} = \dfrac{377.5}{1,200.0} \times 100 = 31.5\%$

QUESTION 2   CALCULATING TRENDS

Product A   Sales quantity and price increase by 10% per year.

Product B   Sales quantity is stable around 500,000, whilst sales price increases yearly by 5%.

Product C   Sales quantity decreases by 10% per year, whilst sales price increases by 10%.

Sales forecasts for 19X6

	Sales Quantity	Sales Price	Sales Revenue
Product A	1,948,717	2.41577	4,707,652
Product B	500,000	12.7629	6,381,450
Product C	59,049	8.0526	475,498

QUESTION 3 ANALYSING SALES ESTIMATES

Salesmen's forecasts less 10%:

	A	B	C
Yorkshire	45,540	72,000	91,080
Lancashire	71,280	231,300	83,160

19X0 sales adjusted by bureau forecasts:

	A	B	C
Yorkshire	46,000	57,500	92,000
Lancashire	72,000	180,000	84,000

These computations show that a correlation does exist between the two forecasts for products A and C. The bureau forecast for product C is approximately 20 per cent lower than the salesmen's forecast.

The discussion should include a consideration of the advantages and disadvantages of the two kinds of forecasts.

QUESTION 4 IDENTIFYING COSTS FROM GRAPHS
(i)

Nature of expense	Graph
1	C
2	F
3	B
4	H
5	E
6	K
7	G
8	D

(ii) Graph A: A cost which is constant up to a certain volume and then increases in proportion to volume, e.g., a subscription to a debt agency which covers a limited number of applications and is then paid at an agreed rate for subsequent applications.

Graph J: A cost which increases per unit at subsequent stages of volume, e.g., similar to (7) above.

£15 for the first 20 tonnes
20 for the next 20 tonnes
25 for the next 20 tonnes

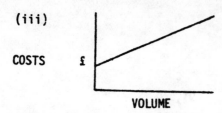

(iii)

COSTS £

VOLUME

This is the graph of a true semi-variable cost, e.g., the cost of power when the tariff is a fixed amount plus a rate for units consumed.

QUESTION 5   CONTRIBUTION MARGIN STATEMENT

(1)

	£	£	£
Sales revenue	80,000	100,000	120,000
Variable costs 60%	48,000	60,000	72,000
Contribution 40%	32,000	40,000	48,000
Fixed costs	30,000	30,000	30,000
Net profit	2,000	10,000	18,000
Per cent of net profit to sales	2.5%	10%	15%

(2) The new approach highlights the importance of cost-colume-profit analysis to profit planning. The conventional profit and loss account is merely an historical document which is unsatisfactory for predictive purposes, e.g., one could not guess that a 20% fall in sales revenue would reduce net profit to 1/5 of its original amount.

QUESTION 6   IDENTIFYING THE ELEMENTS OF A BREAK-EVEN CHART

3   Total cost
4   Variable cost
5   Fixed cost
6   Break-even point
7   Loss
8   Profit
9   Total sales
10   Relevant range

QUESTION 7 ANALYSIS FOR BREAK-EVEN CHART

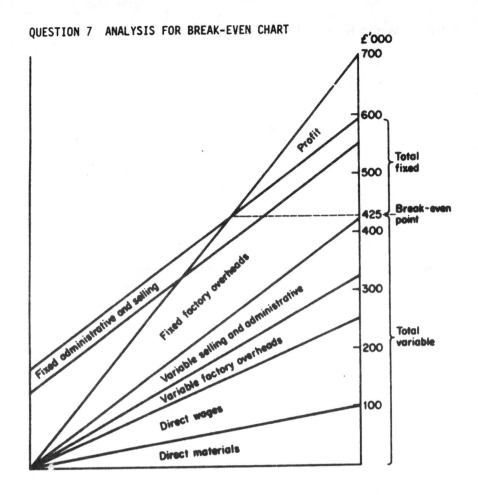

QUESTION 8 THE PROFIT VOLUME CHART

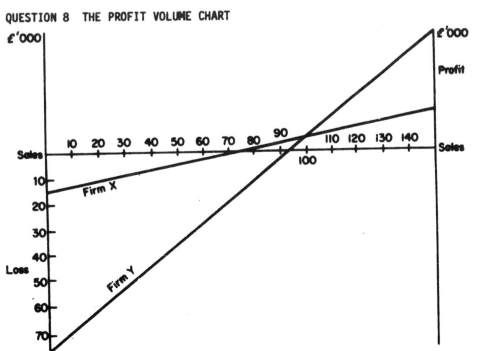

131

Break-even points of the firms can be read from the chart above and may be calculated:

    Firm X £15,000 ÷ 20% = £75,000
    Firm Y £75,000 ÷ 80% = £93,750

Beyond the break-even point, profits increase at different rates. With a low amount of fixed costs to be recovered, Firm X is the first to reach the break-even sales volume. However, its low contribution margin ratio causes profit to accumulate slowly. Because of high fixed costs, Firm Y takes longer to reach the break-even point, but its high contribution margin ratio causes profit to climb rapidly once the break-even sales volume has been attained.

QUESTION 9 GRAPH TO SHOW THE MARGINAL PROFIT SLOPES FOR PRODUCT GROUPS

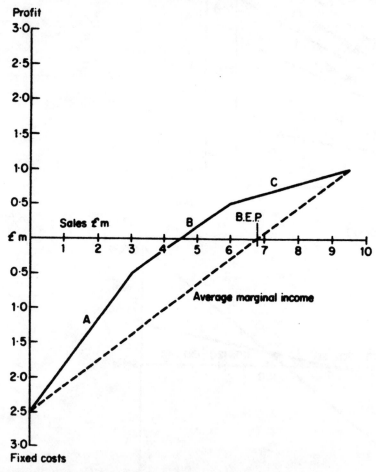

Information to be derived from the graph is:

  (i) The relative profitability of each product group, this being denoted by the steepness of the marginal profit slope. By calculation, the respective P/V ratios are:

132

A (2/3£m) $66\frac{2}{3}$%; B (1/3£m) $33\frac{1}{3}$%; C (1/7£m) $14\frac{2}{7}$%, and for all products combined $\left(\frac{3.5}{9.5} \text{ £m}\right)$ 37%.

On the graph, product group A has the steepest marginal profit slope so is, therefore, the most profitable, a fact borne out by the calculations.

(ii) The break-even point and margin of safety for the combined product groups is shown. This information is, however, valid only while the product mix is as stated.

The conclusions it can be used to illustrate are:

(i) The break-even point is too far to the right of the graph, indicating a too low margin of safety.

(ii) Product groups B and C, which together comprise 2/3rds of the sales, have a marginal profit of only £1.5m, which is insufficient to absorb the fixed costs. This fact is shown on the graph by the marginal income slopes being too gradual. Alternative products should be sought yielding higher contributions.

QUESTION 10 COMPUTATIONS USING PROFIT-VOLUME DATA

(i) Computation of the increase in selling price

$$\text{Increase in selling price} = \frac{\text{Increase in variable labour costs}}{1 - \text{PV ratio}}$$

$$= \frac{\text{Variable labour cost} \times \text{Expected percentage increase in wages}}{\left[1 - \left(\frac{\text{Selling price - Total variable cost}}{\text{Selling price}}\right)\right]}$$

$$= \frac{£12.00 \times 10\%}{\left[1 - \left(\frac{£80.00 - £48.00}{£80.00}\right)\right]}$$

$$= £2.00$$

(ii) Computation of unit volume required

$$\text{Unit volume required} = \frac{\dfrac{\text{Total pound sales volume}}{\text{Selling price}}}{\dfrac{\left[\dfrac{\text{Contribution to fixed costs}}{\text{New PV ratio}}\right]}{\text{Selling price}}}$$

$$= \left[\frac{\left[\dfrac{\text{Present Annual sales volume} \times \text{Profit contribution per unit}}{\text{Selling price} - \left(\dfrac{\text{Total variable cost before wage increase} + \text{Estimated increase in variable labour cost}}{\text{Selling price}}\right)}\right]}{\text{Selling price}}\right]$$

$$= \left| \frac{5,000 \text{ units} \times \pounds32.00}{\left[\dfrac{\pounds80.00 - (\pounds48.00 + \pounds1.20)}{\pounds80.00}\right]} \right|$$

$$= 5,195 \text{ units}$$

(iii) Comparison of estimated net profit before and after capacity increase if the wage increase goes into effect

Estimated net profit before capacity is increased

$$= \left(\begin{array}{c}\text{Current}\\\text{capacity}\end{array} \times \begin{array}{c}\text{Selling}\\\text{price}\end{array} \times \begin{array}{c}\text{New PV}\\\text{ratio}\end{array}\right) - \begin{array}{c}\text{Current}\\\text{fixed costs}\end{array}$$

$$= (5,300 \text{ units} \times \pounds80.00 \times 38.5\%) - \pounds51,000$$

$$= \pounds112,240$$

Estimated net profit after capacity is increased

$$= \left(\begin{array}{c}\text{Current}\\\text{capacity}\end{array} \times \begin{array}{c}\text{New capacity as}\\\text{percentage of}\\\text{current capacity}\end{array} \times \begin{array}{c}\text{Selling}\\\text{Price}\end{array} \times \begin{array}{c}\text{New}\\\text{PV}\\\text{ratio}\end{array}\right) \left(\begin{array}{c}\text{Current}\\\text{fixed}\\\text{costs}\end{array} + \begin{array}{c}\text{Increase}\\\text{in fixed}\\\text{costs}\end{array}\right)$$

$$= (\pounds5,300 \text{ units} \times 130\% \times \pounds80.00 \times 38.5\%)$$

$$- (\pounds51,000 + \pounds19,000)$$

$$= \pounds142,212$$

QUESTION 11 DETERMINATION OF SELLING PRICE
Wellstyled Dress Manufacturing Company

Unit Selling Price £	No. of Dresses	Costs Variable £	Fixed £	Total £	Sales Revenue £	Profit £
14	2,000	14,400	2,400	16,800	28,000	11,200
13	2,600	18,720	2,400	21,120	33,800	12,680
12	3,000	21,600	2,400	24,000	36,000	12,000
11	4,000	28,800	2,400	31,200	44,000	12,800
10	5,000	36,000	2,400	38,400	50,000	11,600

The selling price per dress should be fixed at £11.

QUESTION 12 CONTRIBUTION MARGIN STATEMENTS FROM PROBABILITY DATA
(i)(1) Commercial Products Corporation: Schedule computing the probability of unit sales per month

Unit Sales per Month	Number of Months	Probability
4,000	6	6/30 = 0.2
5,000	15	15/30 = 0.5
6,000	9	9/30 = 0.3
	30	1.0

(2) Schedule of contribution margin for various combinations of unit sales and units manufactured

Unit Sales	Units Manufactured (and Purchased)		
	4,000	5,000	6,000
4,000	£60,000 (1)	£35,000 (2)	£10,000 (2)
5,000	55,000 (3)	75,000 (1)	50,000 (2)
6,000	50,000 (3)	70,000 (3)	90,000 (1)

Notes:

   (1) When all units manufactured are sold:
       4,000 × (£40 - £25) = £60,000
       5,000 × (£40 - £25) = £75,000
       6,000 × (£40 - £25) = £90,000

   (2) Reduction per 1,000 units when more units are manufactured than are sold:
       1,000 × £25 = £25,000

   (3) Reduction per 1,000 units when units must be purchased to fill sales orders:
       1,000 × (£40 - (£40 + £5)) = £5,000

(3) Schedule computing expected contribution margin if 5,000 units are manufactured and all sales orders are filled

Unit Sales	Probability	Contribution Margin	Expected Value
4,000	0.2	£35,000	£ 7,000
5,000	0.5	75,000	37,500
6,000	0.3	70,000	21,000
Expected average monthly contribution margin			£65,500

(ii)(1) Computation of contribution margin if 5,000 units are manufactured with substitute ingredient and all sales orders are filled

Unit Sales	Marginal
4,000 × (£40 - (£25 - £12 + £18)) - 1,000 × (£25 - £12 + £18) =	£ 5,000
5,000 × (£40 - (£25 - £12 + £18)) =	45,000
(6,000 × £40) - (5,000(£25 - £12 + £18) + (1,000 × £45) =	40,000

(2) Schedule computing expected contribution margin with probability of strike at supplier's plant and all sales orders filled

Expected marginal income from manufacturing	165,000
Probability of no strike (1 - 0.6)	0.4
Expected value from manufacturing	26,000
Expected marginal loss from purchasing if strike occurs	125,000
Probability of strike	0.6
Expected loss	(15,000)
Expected contribution margin	£11,000

(3) For the safest alternative the Corporation should order the substitute ingredient during the anticipated strike period because the expected value in contribution margin is greater. (There is a 40 per cent chance that ordering the primary ingredient would product the expected £65,000 contribution margin income but a 60 per cent chance that it would produce a £25,000 marginal loss. Thus the net expectation is £11,000 contribution margin compared to £35,000 from manufacturing using the substitute ingredient.)

(4) Yes, purchase the compound from the competitor. The total future profit which might be lost from losing a customer cannot be estimated, but it is estimated that 80 per cent of the customers would not again buy from the Corporation if orders were refused. Thus the Corporation must weigh losing £5 per unit currently against losing £25 variable production cost on unsold future units plus the loss of the contribution margin on those sales and on any other products which those customers might order.

QUESTION 13 COMPREHENSIVE BUDGETING
(1) Sales Budget

	Units	Selling Price	Revenue
		£	£
Product A	4,000	30	120,000
Product B	2,500	40	100,000
			220,000

(2) Production Budget

	Products	
	A	B
Planned sales	4,000	2,500
Desired closing finished goods stock	1,100	500
Total required	5,100	3,000
Less Opening finished goods stock	100	1,000
Units of production required	5,000	2,000

(3) Direct Materials Used Budget

	Product A			Product B			Total
	Material Content (units)	Production	Usage	Material Content (units)	Production	Usage	Total Usage
Material X	2	5,000	10,000	4	2,000	8,000	18,000
Material Y	1	5,000	5,000	2	2,000	4,000	9,000

	Cost per unit	Cost of materials used
Material X	£3.00	£54,000
Material Y	£1.00	£ 9,000
		63,000

(4) Direct Materials Purchases Budget

	Material X	Material Y
Desired closing stock (units)	8,000	2,000
Units needed for production	18,000	9,000
Total required	26,000	11,000
Less Opening stock	6,000	1,000
Purchases required (units)	20,000	10,000
Price per unit	£3.00	£1.00
Purchase cost	£60,000	£10,000

(5) Direct Labour Budget

	Labour content in product (hours)	Units produced	Total labour hours	Rate per hour	Total Labour cost
				£	£
Machining Dept.					
Product A	2	5,000	10,000	2.00	20,000
Product B	1	2,000	2,000	2.00	4,000
			12,000		
Finishing Dept.					
Product A	1	5,000	5,000	3.00	15,000
Product B	1	2,000	2,000	3.00	6,000
			7,000		45,000
			19,000		

(6) Factory Overhead Cost Budgets

	Machining Dept. at expected 12,000 direct labour hours		Finishing Dept. at expected 7,000 direct labour hours	
	Fixed	Variable	Fixed	Variable
	£	£	£	£
Indirect labour	7,000	-	3,000	-
Indirect material	-	3,000	-	9,000
Repairs	2,000	1,000	500	500
Rates	6,000	-	1,000	-
Depreciation	8,000	-	2,000	-
Heat and light	-	1,000	-	500
Power	1,000	1,000	500	500
	24,000	6,000	7,000	10,500
Rate per direct labour hour	£2.00	£0.50	£1.00	£1.50

(7) Estimated Unit Cost to Manufacture

		Product A		Product B	
	Unit Cost	Units in product	Cost	Units in product	Cost
	£		£		£
Material X	3.00	2	6.00	4	12.00
Material Y	1.00	1	1.00	2	2.00
Direct labour: Machining	2.00	2	4.00	1	2.00
Finishing	3.00	1	3.00	1	3.00
Factory overhead					
Machining - fixed	2.00	2	4.00	1	2.00
- variable	0.50	2	1.00	1	0.50
Finishing - fixed	1.00	1	1.00	1	1.00
- variable	1.50	1	1.50	1	1.50
			21.50		24.00

(8) Closing Stock Budgets

	Units	Unit Cost £	Total Amount £	
Direct materials				
X	8,000	3.00	24,000	
Y	2,000	1.00	2,000	26,000
Finished products				
A	1,100	21.50	23,650	
B	500	24.00	12,000	36,650
				61,650

(9) Cost of Goods Sold Budget

Direct materials used (3)	63,000
Direct labour (5)	45,000
Factory overhead (6)	47,500
	155,500
Add finished goods, opening stock	40,000
	195,500
Less finished goods, closing stock (8)	35,650
	159,850

(10) Selling and Administration Expense Budget

	£	£
__Selling__		
Salaries	10,000	
Advertising	4,000	14,000
__Administration__		
Office salaries	12,000	
Sundry	4,150	16,150
		30,150

(11) Budgeted Cash Flows (for the year as a whole)

	£	£
Cash balance, opening		10,00
Add receipts		210,000
Total cash available		220,000

Less Payments:	£	£
Purchases (4)	70,000	
Direct labour (5)	45,000	
Factory overhead (excluding depreciation) (6)	37,500	
Selling and administration (10)	30,150	
Tax	10,000	
Machinery purchase	20,000	212,650
Closing cash balance		7,350

(12) Budgeted Profit and Loss Account

	£
Sales (1)	220,000
Cost of goods sold (9)	159,850
Gross margin	60,150
Selling and administration expenses	30,150
Net profit before tax	30,000
Tax (50%)	15,000
Net profit after tax	15,000

(13) Budgeted Balance Sheet

	Cost	Provision for Depreciation		
	£	£	£	£
Fixed Assets				
Plant and machinery	220,000	60,000	160,000	
Current Assets				
Raw materials		26,000		
Finished goods		35,650		
Debtors		25,000		
Cash		7,350		
Less: Current liabilities		94,000		
Creditors	8,000			
Tax outstanding	15,000	23,000		
Net current assets			71,000	
				231,000
Capital and reserves				
Share capital			200,000	
Profit and loss account			31,000	
				231,000

QUESTION 14   NEWGEAR ENGINEERING COMPANY LTD

Bank Account 19X8	July £000s	August £000s	September £000s	October £000s	November £000s	December £000s
Receipts						
Balance b/fd	192	264.4	301.6	294.2	279.4	317.2
Debtors	190	168	176	168	190	240
	382	432.4	477.6	462.2	469.4	557.2
Payments:						
Selling and distribution	7	6.4	28	30	32	14
Raw materials	72	80	90	110	80	60
Wages	19.6	21	26	20.8	18	14
Production overhead	12.2	12.6	14	17.2	16.2	11.8
Admin. overhead	4.8	4.8	4.6	4.8	6	5.2
New equipment	22					172
Dividend		46				
Redemption of debentures			20.8			
Balance c/fd	264.4	301.6	294.2	279.4	317.2	280.2
	382	432.4	477.6	462.2	469.4	557.2

QUESTION 15 XYZ ENGINEERING CO. LTD

Cash Budget - September to December 19X2

		Sept £000s	Oct £000s	Nov £000s	Dec £000s
Receipts:					
Balance	b/d	326			
Debtors		300	300	300	300
Parent Co - Loan					44
Balance	c/d	80	96	178	200
		706	396	478	544
Payments:					
Balance	b/d		80	96	178
Creditors - goods		170	140	200	200
Wages - selling and establishment expenses		48	66	72	72
Rent		24	-	-	24
Administration		44	50	50	50
Advertising		20	60	60	20
New plant		400	-	-	-
		706	396	478	544

Monthly Profit and Loss Accounts	Sept £000s	Oct £000s	Nov £000s	Dec £000s
Sales	300	300	320	500
Opening stock	230	190	210	218
Purchases	140	200	200	200
	370	390	410	418
Closing stock	190	210	218	118
Cost of sales	180	180	192	300
Gross margin = 40%	120	120	128	200
Less:				
Wages, etc.	48	72	72	72
Rent	8	8	8	8
Administration expenses	44	50	50	50
Advertising	20	60	60	20
Depreciation	14	14	14	14
	134	204	204	164
Loss/profit per month	(14)	(84)	(76)	36

Net loss £138

Balance Sheet (Forecast) for 31 December 19X8

	£000s	£000s	£000s
Plant and machinery at cost			1,600
Depreciation			584
			1,016
Current Assets			
Investments		250	
Stock		118	
Debtors		820	
		1,188	
Less Current liabilities			
Creditors	218		
Bank overdraft	200	418	770
			1,786
Issued share capital			1,400
Reserves		200	
Retained earnings (£280 - £138)		142	342
			1,742
Parent company loan			44
			1,786

QUESTION 16 FIXED AND FLEXIBLE BUDGETS

(i) Smith's report should contain the following points:

(1) Fixed budgets are poor control instruments, because, owing to the nature of variable costs, total cost incurred varies with output.

(2) Variations from the fixed budget are:

Units of output	<u>1500</u>
Direct materials	£1980
Direct labour	50
Factory supplies	(50)
Indirect labour	16
Repairs etc.	(50)
Insurance	5
	<u>£1951</u>

The conclusions from the above report are favourable. It appears that substantial savings have been made in material costs and smaller savings in direct and indirect labour, and insurance. Small losses occurred in factory supplies and repairs but these appear to be minor. Overall, the report appears favourable and shows a net saving of £1951.

(3) This simplicity is the weakness of the fixed budget. The production budget was not met. The question then is: how much of the above variations is due to the difference in volume? No conclusions can be made regarding this question unless further information is given as to the variability of certain cost elements within the volume. The variable elements are calculated below:

Output = 75,000 units	Budget Total	Fixed Element	Variable Element	Variable rate per unit of output
	£	£	£	£
Direct materials	39,000		39,000	0.52
Direct labour	6,000		6,000	0.08
Factory supplies	1,500		1,500	0.02
Indirect labour	726	126	600	0.008
Repairs etc.	2,250	750	1,500	0.02
Insurance	335	55	300	0.004
Rates	2,000	2,000	-	-
Depreciation	<u>2,200</u>	<u>1,000</u>	<u>1,200</u>	<u>0.16</u>
	54,031	3,931	50,100	0.668

(ii) Using these calculations, the following is obtained:

	Actual Cost of Production	Total Budget Allowance	Original Budget	Total Variation	Expense Variation	Volume Variation
	£	£	£	£	£	£
	(1)	(2)	(3)	(4)	(5)	(6)
Finished units	73,500	73,500	75,000	1,500		
Direct materials	37,020	38,220	39,000	1,980	1,200	780
Direct labour	5,950	5,880	6,000	50	(70)	120
Factory supplies	1,550	1,470	1,500	(50)	(80)	30
Indirect labour	710	714	726	16	4	12
Repairs etc.	2,300	2,220	2,250	(50)	(80)	30
Insurance	350	349	355	5	(1)	6
Rates	2,000	2,000	2,000	-	-	-
Depreciation	2,200	2,176	2,200	-	(24)	24
	52,080	53,029	54,031	1,951	949	1,002

A comparison of columns (4) and (5) illustrates the misleading nature of fixed budgets which conceal changes in cost due to volume changes. A gain of £50 for direct labour is in actual fact a loss of £70.

(4) An important conclusion which emerges from the above example is that the flexible budget alone will not supply all the answers we require for evaluating performance. For example, does the gain on direct material costs represent lower prices or lower material usage? Smith, in installing flexible budgets for cost control, should indicate that this requires costs to be analysed within the framework of organizational responsibility. If the manager of a dept. is to make effective use of a budget for control purposes, it not only must be flexible but must give recognition to the extent to which he is able to influence costs identified with his department. Overhead variance analysis based upon a standard costing system enables extension of the analysis in this way.

Chapter 12

QUESTION 1   USING RELEVANT COST DATA

Course A - sell for scrap		£6,500
Course B - sales (8,000 × £3.20)		£25,600
Less: variable costs		
(8,000 × £2)		£16,000
		£ 9,600

Fixed costs are irrelevant

Course C - $8,000 \times (1.20 \times 1.5) \times \frac{5}{800}$ = £9,000

(1)   Select course B

(2)   The opportunity cost is £9,000

(3)   The cash flow that can arise or be saved in future as a consequence of the decision constitutes the relevant data.

(4)   The sunk costs in this example are:

    (a)   the original purchase of the material

    (b)   the labour costs involved in making the figurines

    (c)   the fixed costs which are part of the basis of the absorption costing system.

QUESTION 2

Relevant cost data

1(a)   Incremental cost of the order is:

Costs incurred to fill order *	£
Material	10,000
Labour	18,000
Special overhead	2,000
	30,000

* Depreciation, rent and heat and light are not affected by the order. Power might be depending upon the particular requirements of the special units. It is assumed here that the same amount of power will be used in each case.

Costs reduced for standard products	£
Material	4,000
Labour	4,500
Other	450
	8,950
Total Incremental Costs	21,050

(b) The full cost of the order is:

	£
Costs incurred to fill order (from 1)	30,000
Depreciation	1,800
Power	200
Rent	500
Heat and light	50
	32,550

(c) The opportunity cost of taking the order is the net cash flow given up.

	£
Sales of standard product	12,500
Less: Material	4,000
Labour	4,500
Power	200
Other	450
	9,150
Opportunity cost of special order	3,350

(d) The sunk costs are the costs that don't change as a result of choosing one order or the other.

	£
Depreciation	1,800
Power	200
Rent	500
Heat and light	50
	2,550

2. On the basis of the data in the question it would pay Jackson to accept the order.

	£	£
New sales	35,000	
Less: Standard sales	12,500	
		22,500
Incremental costs (A.1)		21,050
Cash advantage to Special Units		1,450

Other factors must be considered such as the long-run consequences of failing to satisfy standard parts customers, the reliability of the cost estimates and the importance of this valued customer.

QUESTION 3 DECISIONS USING RELEVANT COST DATA

(1) In any situation where a 'make-or-buy' decision is involved, only those costs which will differ among alternatives are relevant. Fixed costs, by definition, are unavoidable within the range of planning and operation. Variable costs are thus the only costs to be considered.

	Per Unit	
	Part A4	Part B5
	£	£
Standard cost	5.40	14.70
Less: Fixed factory overhead costs		
Part A4: 60% × £4.00	(2.40)	
Part B5: 60% × £2.00		(1.20)
Relevant (Variable) costs	3.00	13.50

Alternatively, the variable cost for each part could be computed as follows:

	Per Unit	
	Part A4	Part B5
Direct materials	0.40	8.00
Direct labour	1.00	4.70
Variable factory overhead		
Part A4: 40% × £4.00	1.60	
Part B5: 40% × £2.00		0.80
Relevant (Variable) costs	3.00	13.50

(2) Since allocation of machine hours to production of either or both of the parts is to be based upon cost savings per machine hour, it follows that we should allocate the maximum number of hours necessary to the product which has greater potential savings. The remaining hours would then be allocated to the product which has a lesser cost savings per hour.

We first compute the savings per unit as a result of manufacturing rather than buying. This savings is then divided by the number of hours required to produce a unit in order to determine the savings per machine hour:

	Per Unit	
	Part A4	Part B5
	£	£
Cost to purchase	5.00	15.00
Variable costs to manufacture (see solution to question 2)	(3.00)	(13.50)
(i) Cost savings if manufactured	2.00	1.50
(ii) Machine hours required to manufacture	4	2
(iii) Savings per machine hour % (i)/(ii)	0.50	0.75

It appears desirable to produce as many Parts B5 as necessary and then use any excess hours to produce Part A4.

Total machine hours available		30,000
Part B5:		
(i) Units needed per year	8,000	
(ii) Hours required per unit	2	
Total hours required: (i) × (ii)		(16,000)
(iii) Excess hours available to product Part A4		14,000
Part A4:		
(iv) Hours required per unit	4	
Maximum possible production: (iii)/(iv)	3,500	
Total hours used		(14,000)
		- 0 -

Therefore, the company should produce 8,000 units of Part B5 and 3,500 units of Part A4 in the year 19X5.

QUESTION 4 PRODUCT CONTRIBUTION MARGINS

(1) The Marcia Company Contribution margin of a Unit of Each Product

Item	Sales Price	Variable Costs Material	Labour	Overhead	Total	Contribution Margin
	£	£	£	£	£	£
Laurie	5.20	1.40	0.80	0.40	2.60	2.60
Debbie	2.40	0.70	0.50	0.25	1.45	0.95
Sarah	8.50	2.69	1.40	0.70	4.79	3.71
Kathy	4.00	1.00	1.00	0.50	2.50	1.50
Sewing kit						
Regular	3.00	0.60	0.40	0.20	1.20	1.80
Reduced	2.55	0.60	0.40	0.20	1.20	1.35

(2) Contribution margin per Labour Pound Expended on Each Product

	Contribution Margin per Unit	Labour Cost per Unit	Contribution Margin per Labour £
	£	£	£
Laurie	2.60	0.80	3.25
Debbie	0.95	0.50	1.90
Sarah	3.71	1.40	2.65
Kathy	1.50	1.00	1.50
Sewing kit			
Regular	1.80	0.40	4.50
Reduced	1.35	0.40	3.38

(3) Total Hours Required to Produce Estimated Sales Units

Item	Esimated Unit Sales	Labour Hours per Unit	Total Labour Hours
Laurie	50,000	80/200	20,000
Debbie	42,000	50/200	10,500
Sarah	35,000	140/200	24,500
Kathy	40,000	100/200	20,000
Sewing kit	325,000	40/200	65,000
Total hours required			140,000
Effective productive capacity			130,000
Hours required in excess of effective productive capacity			10,000

Since the Kathy doll produces the lowest profit contribution per labour hour, it should be recommended that its production be reduced by 20,000 units (10,000 ÷ 100/200).

(4) The possible methods of providing the estimated missing productive capacity of 12,000 labour hours or 24,000 Kathy dolls include the following:

(a) The company may resort to employing its labour on an overtime basis. During the overtime periods, a premium of 50% of the base labour rate would be paid. Assuming that the variable costs are related directly to the labour costs, the cost of producing a Kathy doll on an overtime basis would be:

Material	£1.00
Labour	1.50
Variable overhead	0.75
	£3.25

The selling price of £4.00 per doll results in a contribution to profit of £0.75. Also to be considered is whether fixed costs and the rate for the application of the variable overhead will change as a result of the extended use of personnel and facilities. In addition, the effect of the overtime on labour efficiency would be determined.

(b) The production of the 24,000 Kathy dolls needed to fill the estimated sales figures may be contracted out to another manufacturer. In this case the main factor would be the contract price per doll. If the contract price did not exceed the difference between the £4.00 selling price and the added handling costs, a contribution would be made to total profit.

(c) The company may expand facilities and equipment to attain the increased output of 12,000 hours. Here the factors to be weighed include the cost of the expansion, the expectations as to sales volume in subsequent years, and the cost of training additional personnel.

(d) The company may give thought to installing a second shift. This move does not appear to be a feasible alternative because the needed output represents a minor amount of the total productive capacity.

QUESTION 5 DECISION-MAKING USING LIMITING FACTORS

		£
Barley	100 acres	
Yield @ 1.50 tonnes per acre - 150 tonnes @ £25 per tonne		3,750
Variable costs	per acre	
Seed	£2.50	
Fertilizer	£3.50	600
	Contribution	3,150
	Contribution per acre	31.5

151

Dairy <u>20 acres kale & 80 acres grazing</u> or <u>100 acres grazing</u>

	(40 cows)			(50 cows)	
Output		£			£
40 calves		400	50 calves		500
Milk (40 × £120)		4,800	(50 × £120)		6,000
		5,200			6,500
Variable costs					
Kale	per acre		Purchased		£
Seed	£2		50 × £12.50		625
Fertilizers	£5		Feeding stuffs		1,250
	—		'Depreciation'		500
	£7				
		£			
× 20		140			
Feeding stuffs		1,000			
'Depreciation'		400	1,540		2,375
Contribution			3,660		4,125
Contribution per acre			£36.6		£41.25

The nominal yield from growing kale would be as follows:

Value of output	40 × £12.50		£500
Variable cost		£	
Seed	20 × £2	40	
Fertilizer	20 × £5	100	£140
Contribution			360
Contribution per acre			£18.0

The above figures indicate:

(1) Kale should not be grown as its nominal contribution rate is low.

(2) Use of land for dairy farming gives a higher contribution than growing barley. Therefore, maximum profit will be attained, if barley is not discontinued because of its lower yield, as follows:

				£
Barley	100 acres	Contribution		3,150
Dairy	100 acres	"		4,125
				7,275
Fixed farm costs		£		
Wages		1,800		
Rent, rates, etc.		1,200		
General charges		3,000		6,00'
			Net profit	1,275

QUESTION 6   MAKE OR BUY DECISIONS

(1)   Comparison of precision machinery department costs:

	With manufacture of Factrons	Factrons purchased from Supplier
	£	£
Materials	67,500	50,000
Direct labour	50,000	22,000
Indirect labour	20,000	14,000
Light and heat	5,500	5,500
Power	3,000	2,700
Depreciation	10,000	8,000
Property taxes and insurance	8,000	7,000
Payroll taxes and other benefits (14% of labour costs)	9,800	5,040
Other	5,000	4,500
Additional cost resulting from outside purchase:		
Material		40,000
Freight		2,500
Indirect labour		5,000
Payroll taxes and other benefits		700
	178,800	166,940

(2)   Items to be considered by management in its decision on whether to make or buy Factrons:

(a)   Purchases from outside would result in annual savings of approximately £12,000.

(b)   The disposition of machinery would provide additional working capital.

(c)   Would the elimination of manufacturing Factrons upset present production schedules of the department and result in slack periods within the department?

(d)   Can the plant area occupied by Factron production be effectively utilized in other production?

(e)   Is the supplier adequately capitalized? Are the supplier's production facilities adequate to maintain a production schedule that will minimize the investment in stock or will there be an increase in the investment in stock? If a large stock is required, would plant area be available for the larger quantity?

(f)   What is the supplier's reputation among its customers as to meeting production schedules?

(g)   Would the quality standards of the outside supplier be equal to those of the department?

(h) Would the supplier's price and production requirements be fixed by contracts? What is the potential for obsolescence which might give rise to the required purchase due to a contract of obsolete parts?

(i) Should the company rely on only one supplier or should the work be distributed to two suppliers in order to protect against interruptions due to strikes or other delays? Would the original supplier's quotation be increased if the work was distributed between two suppliers rather than going to only one supplier?

QUESTION 7 MAKE OR BUY
Atrix Ltd
(a) Revised Statements of Comparison

	Manufacture £	Buying £
Cost of crates		33,600
Materials	16,000	
Specialized labour	6,400	
Variable overhead	1,600	
	24,000	33,600

The costs used in the revised statement for manufacturing are the relevant ones for the decisions.

(1) General Labour

Since the costing system has allocated this, it is presumed that the labour is drawn from a larger pool and is not, therefore, dismissed if not engaged on crate manufacture.

(2) Supervisory Labour

Once again this is an allocated expense already committed and hence plays no part in any future decision.

(3) Fixed Overhead

As an allocated part of already committed expense, this too does not come into the calculation. It is possible that a 'buy' decision may allow the special crate machinery to be sold which would give rise to a once only cash inflow.

It can be seen, then, that the decision which produces the least cash outflows in future is the one to manufacture and not the one to buy.

(b) The benefits of manufacture may well also include
(1) Control over delivery dates
(2) Control over quality
(3) Security of long run supply
(4) Opportunity to sell surpluses
(5) Opportunity to diversity

154

Some of these factors could outweigh a cash advantage where the external price quoted is lower than relevant manufacturing costs.

Equally, buying advantages over manufacture generally may be

(1) No need to engage in expensive research

(2) No need to employ specialist additional staff

(3) Ability to concentrate on own expertise

Naturally many of these features may become obvious as cash factors in the original decision model.

QUESTION 8 THE 'SELL OR FURTHER PROCESS' DECISION

Present output at standard

Sales	Tonnes	Selling Prices	Total Sales
			£
Product A	1,000	£150 per tonne	150,000
Product B	500	£100 per tonne	50,000
Product C	600	£ 50 per tonne	30,000
			230,000

Standard Costs	£	
Direct materials	70,000	
Direct wages	30,000	
Variable overheads	45,000	
Fixed overheads	60,000	205,000
Budgeted profit		25,000

Revised output at standard

Sales			
Original value			230,000
		£	
Additional value	A	20,000	
	B	12,000	
	C	15,000	47,000
			277,000

Standard costs			£	
Original			205,000	

Additional	A £	B £	C £		
Material	10,000	3,000	7,000		
Labour	4,000	2,000	2,000		
Variable overhead	6,000	3,000	3,000		
	20,000	8,000	12,000	40,000	245,000
	Budgeted Profit				32,000

155

Summary of additional profit

	A £	B £	C £	Total £
Incremental sales	20,000	12,000	15,000	47,000
Incremental cost	20,000	8,000	12,000	40,000
Incremental profit	-	4,000	3,000	7,000
% profit to sales	-	$33\frac{1}{3}$%	20%	15%

From the above information it is recommended that:

(1) Further processing of Product A should not be carried out, unless there are undisclosed reasons, because it does not add to the net profit. The spare capacity should be utilized in other directions.

(2) As between products B and C the reprocessing of B is the more advantageous and should be undertaken to the maximum extent. If this is possible without loss of facilities in respect of C the further processing of both should be carried out in order to attain the highest profit.

QUESTION 9 DROPPING A PRODUCT LINE

Eastern Company - Contribution of Product C to fixed costs and expenses

	£	£	£
Sales			350,000
Less variable costs and expenses:			
Production:			
Raw materials	80,000		
Direct labour	150,000		
Fringe benefits (15% of direct labour)	22,500		
Royalties	3,500		
Factory supplies	2,100		
Electrical power	3,000		
Scrap and spoilage	600	261,700	
Selling:			
Sales commissions	15,000		
Fringe benefits	2,250		
Delivery expense	10,000		
Advertising expense	26,000	53,250	314,950
Contribution of product C to fixed costs and expenses			35,050

QUESTION 10 'SPECIAL ORDER' PRICING

(1)(a) An increase in profit of £1,200 (before taxes) would result from accepting the £15,000 offer.

(b) The minimum price needed to have no effect on profits is £13,800.

$$\frac{\text{Variable overhead}}{\text{Total overhead}} = \text{Percent Overhead Variable}$$

$$\frac{£60,000}{150,000} = 40\%$$

Overhead Rate × Percent Overhead Variable =

Variable Overhead Rate per Direct labour

25% × 40% = 10%

	£
Variable costs of quoted boat	
Direct material	5,000
Direct labour	8,000
Variable Overhead (10% × 8,000)	800
	13,800
Customer's offer	15,000
Variable costs	13,800
Contribution to profit	1,200

(2) The contribution margin approach focuses on the relationship between the costs to be incurred as a result of taking an order and the revenue the order will produce. The impact of a specific order on profits can be estimated and the lower limits on price can be observed.

(3) The major pitfall to the contribution margin approach to pricing is its failure to explicitly recognize the fixed costs. Although they can be over-looked in the short-run, the fixed costs must be covered in the long-run if the business is to continue.

QUESTION 11 THE ANALYSIS OF A FIRM'S ACTIVITIES

	Printing Dept. Last Year	Printing Dept. Without Printing	Shipping Dept. Last Year	Shipping Dept. Without Printing
	£	£	£	£
Salaries and wages	150,000	17,000	25,000	3,000
Telephone and telegraph	3,700	1,250	300	250
Materials and supplies	250,000	-	10,000	5,000
Occupancy costs	80,000	30,000	10,000	10,000
General and administrative costs	30,000	25,000	4,000	4,000
Depreciation	40,000	-	5,000	-
	553,700	73,250	54,300	22,250
	73,250		22,250	
Net decrease	480,450		32,050	

	£
	£
Total decrease per above	512,500
Other adjustments:	
Publishing dept. clerk required	(4,000)
Interest reduction from application of net funds released	13,000
One-fifth of termination pay offset against each year of contract	(8,000)
Net decrease in cost, without printing	513,500
Cost of outside printing	550,000
Net advantage to continue printing	36,500
Calculation of funds released:	
Proceeds from sale of equipment	300,000
Less - Termination pay ($\frac{1}{4}$ of £133,000 + 22,000 + 5,000)	40,000
Net funds released	260,000
Interest at 5%	13,000

QUESTION 12   CLAMART COMPANY LTD

(1) Objective function

Maximize $2N + 3S$ where N is Normal Service
and S is Super Service

subject to

$4N + 5S \leq 360$ Interior cleaning capacity
$10N + 6S \leq 540$ Exterior cleaning capacity
$N; S; \geq 0$

(Ignoring the problem of the integer solution generally)

(2) See graph page 175

(3) (a) From Graph $N = 60; S = 40$

(b) $4N + 3S = 360$ solve for $S + N$
   $10N + 6S = 540$

(i) $4N + 3S = 360 \times 2 = 720$
   $8N + 6S = 720$
   $- 10N + 6S = 540$
   $3N = 180$
   $N = 60$
$\therefore S = 40$

(2)

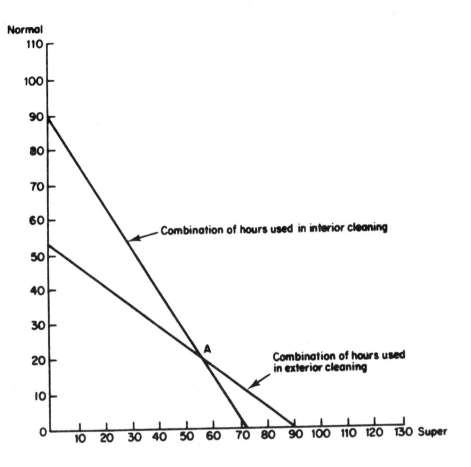

Normal

Combination of hours used in interior cleaning

A

Combination of hours used
in exterior cleaning

Super

QUESTION 13 LINEAR PROGRAMMING

(1) The objective function

Maximize MC = £0.80W + £1.10G + £1.20T

where MC is the total marginal contribution

(2) The capacity constraint

Minutes

4W + 10G + 4T ≤ 10,000 (Milling)

8W + 4G + 8T ≤ 14,000 (Grinding)

4W + 2G + 2T ≤ 10,000 (Painting)

(3) The non-negativity requirements

W ≥ 0

G ≥ 0

T ≥ 0

Chapter 13

QUESTION 1   PREPARING A STANDARD COST SHEET
Standard Cost Sheet
(per 1,000 units)

	60%	80%	100%
	£	£	£
Material X	1,000	800	600
Material Y	2,000	1,800	1,600
Labour - Dept. 1	2,200	2,200	2,200
Dept. 2	2,600	2,600	2,600
Factory overheads	2,000	1,800	1,600
	9,800	9,200	8,600

QUESTION 2   COMPUTING MATERIALS AND LABOUR VARIANCES
Standard Direct Cost per Unit

	£	£
Direct Materials		
DM1 6 kilos @ £1.50 per kilo	9.00	
DM2 10 kilos @ £0.60 per kilo	6.00	15.00
Direct Wages		
Grade A 8 hours @ £1.00 per hour	8.00	
Grade B 5 hours @ £0.80 per hour	4.00	12.00
		27.00

Calculation of Variances
(1)   Direct Materials Cost Variance
   (a)   Materials Price Variance

	£	£
DM1 62,400 kilos @ (£1.50 - £1.40)	6,240 F	
DM2 103,000 kilos @ (0.60 - £0.65)	5,150 F	11,390 F

（b）Materials Usage Variance

DM1	(62,400 - 61,200) kilos @ £1.50 per kilo	1,800 U	
DM2	(103,000 - 102,000) kilos @ £0.60 per kilo	600 U	2,400 U

(c) Direct Materials Cost Variance   8,990 F

(2) Direct Labour Cost Variance

(a) Wage Rate Variance

Grade A	79,800 hours @ (£1.00 - £1.10)	7,980 U	
Grade B	50,500 hours @ (£0.80 - £0.75)	2,525 F	5,455 U

(b) Labour Efficiency Variance

Grade A (79,800 - 81,600) hours @ £1.00 per hour		1,800F	
Grade B (50,500 - 51,000) hours @ £0.80 per hour		400 F	2,200 F

(c) Direct Labour Cost Variance   3,255 U

QUESTION 3   RECORDING STANDARD COSTS

Creditors account

Material price variance	11,390	Stores	155,400

Materials account

Creditors	155,400	Work-in-progress	153,000
		Material usage variance	2,400
	155,400		155,400

Wages account

Cash	125,655	Work-in-progress	122,400
Direct labour efficiency	2,200	Wage rate variance	5,455
	127,855		127,855

Work-in-Progress account

Wages	122,400	Transfer to finished goods	275,400
Materials	153,000		
	275,400		275,400

Material Price Variance account

		Creditors	11,390

Material Usage Variance account

Stores	2,400

Wages   5,455

                                          Wages   2,200

QUESTION 4 CALCULATING MATERIALS AND LABOUR VARIANCES
Direct materials variances

	Product X Kilos used	Product Y Kilos used	Price Difference £	Price variances £	£
Direct materials A	41,000	115,000	(0.65 - 0.6)	2,050 (U)	5,750 (U)
Direct materials B	63,000	29,000	(0.75 - 0.8)	3,150 (F)	1,450 (F)
				1,100 (F)	4,300 (U)

Standard usage

	Product X	Product Y
Direct materials A	1,010 units × 40 kilos = 40,400	1,550 units × 80 kilos = 124,000
Direct materials B	1,010 units × 60 kilos = 60,600	1,550 units × 20 kilos = 31,000

	Product X	Usage variances £
Direct materials A	(41,000 - 40,400) kilos × £0.6 per kilo =	360 (U)
Direct materials B	(63,000 - 60,600) kilos × £0.8 per kilo =	1,920 (U)
		2,280 (U)

	Product Y	
Direct materials A	(115,000 - 124,000) kilos × £0.6 per kilo =	5,400 (F)
Direct materials B	(29,000 - 31,000) kilos × £0.8 per kilo =	1,600 (F)
		7,000 (F)

Direct wages variances

	Product X Hours worked	Product Y Hours worked	Wage rate Difference £	Wage Rate Variances £	£
Cutting	1,950	5,950	(2.0 - 1.9)	195 (F)	595 (F)
Assembling	9,850	7,400	(1.6 - 1.7)	985 (U)	740 (U)
				790 (U)	145 (U)

Standard production times

	Product X	Product Y
Cutting	1,010 × 2 hours = 2,020	1,550 × 4 = 6,200
Assembling	1,010 × 10 hours = 10,100	1,550 × 5 = 7,750

162

	Product X	Efficiency variances
Cutting	(1,950 - 2,020) hours × £2.0 per hour	140 (F)
Assembling	(9,850 -10,100) hours × £1.6 per hour	400 (F)
		540 (F)

	Product Y	
Cutting	(5,950 - 6,200) hours × £2.0 per hour	500 (F)
Assembling	(7,400 - 7,750) hours × £1.6 per hour	560 (F)
		1,060 (F)

QUESTION 5   COMPLETING A PERFORMANCE REPORT

Variable costs	Incurred costs	Budget at standard time allowance	Total variance	Spending variance	Efficiency variance
	£	£	£	£	£
Indirect material	4,700	4,600	100U	-	100U
Inspection	1,750	1,840	90F	130F	40U
Cutting tools	430	460	30F	40F	10U
	6,880	6,900	20F	170F	150U

QUESTION 6   COMPUTING MATERIALS, LABOUR AND OVERHEAD VARIANCES

(a) Bronson Company Schedule to compute cost variances for the month of September 19X0

			£	
1.	Actual cost of materials purchased		1,044,000	
	Materials purchased at standard cost			
	Miracle mix	£1,000,000		
	Drums	94,000	1,094,000	
	Materials price variance		50,000	favourable
2.	Actual materials used at standard cost			
	Miracle mix	£1,300,000		
	Drums	80,000	1,380,000	
	Standard usage (80,000 × £17)		1,360,000	
			20,000	unfavourable
3.	Actual direct labour cost		414,100	
	Actual hours at standard cost (82,000 × £5)		410,000	
	Labour rate variance		4,100	unfavourable

4.	Actual hours at standard cost	410,000	
	Standard hours at standard cost (80,000 × £5)	400,000	
	Labour efficiency variance	10,000	unfavourable
5.	Actual variable overhead	98,000	
	Actual hours worked × V.O.R. (82,000 × £1.125)	92,050	
	Variable overhead spending variance	5,950	unfavourable
6.	Actual hours worked × V.O.R.	92,050	
	Standard hours produced × V.O.R. (80,000 × £1.125)	90,000	
	Variable overhead efficiency variance	2,050	unfavourable
7.	Budgeted overhead	760,000	
	Factory overhead applied	480,000	
	Volume variance	280,000	unfavourable

(b) Bronson Company Schedule to Compute manufacturing Cost per Drum of Product at New Level of Production

New level of production = 140,000 drums   £

Materials:

	£
Miracle mix (8 × £2.10)	16.80
Drum	1.00
	17.80
Direct labour	5.70
Fixed factory overhead	4.00
Variable factory overhead	2.50
	£30.00

QUESTION 7 COMPUTING MATERIALS, LABOUR AND OVERHEAD VARIANCES

(1) Ross Shirts, Ltd

Standard Cost of Production for the month ending October 31

Lot	Quantity	Standard Cost Per Unit £	Total Standard Cost £
30	1,000	26.55	26,550
31	1,700	26.55	45,135
32	1,200	23.88 *	28,656
	Standard Cost of Production		100,341

* Standard material cost plus 80% of standard cost of labour and overhead
(£13.20 + (0.80 × £13.35)).

164

(2) Ross Shirts Ltd Schedule Computing Materials Price Variance for the month ending October 31

	£
Actual cost of materials purchased	53,200
Standard cost of materials purchased (95,000 × £0.55)	52,250
Unfavourable materials price variance	950

(3) Ross Shirts Ltd Schedule of Material and Labour Variances for the month ending October 31

	Total	Lot No. 30	Lot No. 31	Lot No. 32
Materials quantity variance:				
Standard metres:				
Units in lot	3,900	1,000	1,700	1,200
Standard metres per lot	24	24	24	24
Total standard quantity	93,600	24,000	40,800	28,800
Actual metres used	93,365	24,100	40,440	28,825
Variance in metres	(235)	100	(360)	25

	Total	Lot No. 30	Lot No. 31	Lot No. 32
Labour efficiency variance:				
Standard hours:				
Units in lot	3,900	1,000	1,700	1,200
Standard hours	3	3	3	3
Total	11,700	3,000	5,100	3,600
Percentage of completion		100	100	80
Total standard hours	10,980	3,000	5,100	2,890
Actual hours worked	11,000	2,980	5,130	2,890
Variance in hours	20	(20)	30	10

	Total	Lot No. 30	Lot No. 31	Lot No. 32
Labour rate variance:				
Actual hours worked	11,000	2,980	5,130	2,890
Rate paid in excess of standard (£2.50 - £2.45)	£0.05	0.05	0.05	0.05
Variance	£550.00	£149.00	£256.50	£144.50

(4) Ross Shirts, Ltd   Schedule of Overhead Variances for the month ending
October 31 19X9

Variable Overhead Variances	£
Actual variable overhead	13,150
Actual hours worked × S.V.O.R. (11,000 × £1.2)	13,200
Spending variance	(50)
Actual hours worked × S.V.O.R.	13,200
Standard hours production × S.V.O.R. (10,980 × £1.2)	13,176
Efficiency variance	24

Fixed Overhead Variances	
Actual fixed overhead	9,700
Budgeted fixed overhead	9,600
Spending variance	100
Budgeted fixed overhead (12,000 × £0.8)	9,600
Standard hours production × S.F.O.R. (10,980 × £0.8)	8,784
Volume variance	816

Check:

Total overhead variance = (Actual fixed + variable overhead) - (Standard hours produced × variable + fixed overhead rate)

= £22,850 - (10,980 × £2)

= £8,904

( ) denotes favourable variance.

QUESTION 8   SALES VARIANCES

	(a)	(b)	(c)	(d)	(e)	(f)	(g)	(h)
Product	Actual Contribution	Actual Quantity	Standard Contribution Margin	Value	Actual Quantity in Standard Proportions	Standard Contribution	Value	Budgeted Margin
	£	Units	£	£	Units	£	£	£
X	9,000	1,500	6	9,000	2,500	6	15,000	12,000
Y	10,000	2,500	4	10,000	2,500	4	10,000	8,000
Z	14,000	3,500	1	3,500	2,500	1	2,500	2,000
	33,000	7,500		22,500	7,500		27,500	22,000

Sale Price Variance (a) - (d) £10,500 favourable

Sales   (g) - (h)   £ 5,500 favourable

Sales Mix Variance (d) - (g)   £ 5,000 unfavourable

167

Part 3 Case Problems and Analysis
Case Problem 1   T. Albert

(1)   A simple, yet complete double entry system is expected as the answer to this section. Students may well offer some variations as to what would constitute the complete set of appropriate books but a typical set would consist of:

Cash book   } These may be combined in the
Bank account } usual two column approach
General Ledger

Given the present number of transactions it would hardly appear to warrant a separate debtors' ledger.

(2)   See set of accounts, following.

(3)   (a)   The control of cash could be fairly easily managed by the simple expedient of counting the cash in hand at any time and comparing it with the balance shown on the cash account. All supporting evidence of transactions would be required to be kept; e.g., daily till rolls for cash sales, invoices and receipts for expenditure.

The control of the bank would be similarly effected although the usual problems associated with the delay in clearance of cheques and the direct entry of items into bank records would need a supporting reconciliation statement.

(b)   and (d) In this case the volume of transactions concerning debtors and creditors does not appear to warrant further accounting elaboration.

(c)   This form of accounting does not allow any direct independent check on stock. The best that could be hoped for is that, given stable gross margin ratios, a rough check would be available when a profit and loss account is drawn up.

(4) To establish the accuracy of the recording system a trial balance should be extracted as described in the main text. The fact that the sum of debit balance equals the sum of credit balances extracted is only prima facie evidence of accuracy. A trial balance would not reveal the posting of an item to the wrong account nor the omission of a transaction altogether.

(5) (a) Efficiency is a relative term and can only be considered in accounting terms by:
   (i) comparison with other firms engaged in the same trade, and
   (ii) comparison with other uses of the resources (including the proprietor's endeavours) presently committed to this enterprise.
(b) Profit can be conventionally determined by preparation of a Profit and Loss account (See below).
(c) The balance sheet attached reveals the change that has taken place during January (ignoring depreciation). (See below).

(6) Students would be expected to calculate some ratios but the comments in (5) (supra) would still be valid.

(7) The most important decision facing T. Albert at any time is whether to continue in the present business. He would need to know:
   (i) what alternative business opportunities exist;
   (ii) what rate of interest is available if capital were to be invested in securities, banks or other institutions;
   (iii) what employment he could obtain.
Obviously the accounting results do not attempt to reveal this data but merely present a conventional view of profit against which the above information can be used.

Students may be expected to raise the problems regarding the use of conventions and the limitations engendered by their use.

Cash account

19X7			£	19X7			£
Jan	1	Bank - Float	40	Jan	3	Wages	28
"	2	Sales	45	"	5	Bank	200
"	3	"	112	"	8	Returns - Sales	12
"	5	"	82	"	11	Wages	28
"	9	"	56				
"	12	"	114	"	16	Bank	200
"	14	"	74	"	19	Wages	28
"	16	"	28	"	22	Cleaning	13
"	19	"	208	"	23	Postages	5
"	21	"	38	"	24	Bank	150
"	22	"	142	"	25	Wages	28
"	24	"	16	"	28	Tea, milk, etc.	10
"	25	"	23	"	30	Drawings	60
"	26	"	51	"	30	Wages	28
"	28	"	15	"	31	Balance c/d	435
"	29	"	49				
"	30	"	37				
"	31	"	95				
			1,225				1,225
Feb	1	Balance b/d	435				

Bank account

19X7			£	19X7			£
Jan	1	Amount introduced	15,000	Jan	1	Rent	625
"	5	Cash	200	"	1	Cash	40
"	16	Cash	200	"	2	Insurance	24
"	21	Bilden Const. Co. Ltd	150	"	10	Goods purchased	2,140
"	24	Cash	150	"	14	Electricity	18
				"	14	Advertising	39
				"	17	Drawings	50
				"	18	Rates	240
				"	25	Unac W.C. Ltd	1,500
				"	29	Tracas Fabrics Ltd	1,600
				"	31	Balance c/d	9,424
			15,700				15,700
19X7							
Feb	1	Balance b/d	9,424				

Sales account

19X7			£	19X7			£
Jan	8	Cash	12	Jan	2	Cash	45
"	31	Balance c/d	1,733	"	3	"	112
				"	5	"	82
				"	9	"	56
				"	9	Newgate Edn. Authority	210
				"	12	Cash	114
				"	14	"	74
				"	15	Bilden Constr. Co. Ltd	350
				"	16	Cash	28
				"	19	"	208
				"	21	"	38
				"	22	"	142
				"	24	"	16
				"	25	"	23
				"	26	"	51
				"	28	"	15
				"	29	"	49
				"	30	"	37
				"	31	"	95
			1,745				1,745
				19X7			
				Feb	1	Balance	1,733

Purchases account

19X7		£	19X7		£
Jan 1	Unac	2,500	Jan 8	Returns	120
" 3	Tracas	1,600	" 31	Bal. c/d	6,120
" 10	Bank	2,140			
		6,240			6,240
19X7					
Feb 1	Bal. b/d	6,120			

Unac Wholesale Co. Ltd

19X7		£	19X7		£
Jan 1	Returns	120	Jan 1	Goods	2,500
" 26	Bank	1,500			
" 31	Bal. c/d	880			
		2,500			2,500
			Feb 1	Bal. b/d	880

Tracas Fabric Ltd

19X7		£	19X7		£
Jan 29	Bank	1,600	Jan 3	Goods	1,600

Fixture and Fittings account

19X7		£
Jan 2	Evron	500

Evron Fittings Ltd

			19X7		£
			Jan 2	Goods	500

Rent and Rates account

19X7		£	19X7		£
Jan 1	Bank	625	Jan 31	Bal. c/d	865
" 18	Bank	240			
		865			865
19X7					
Feb 1	Bal. b/d	865			

Insurance account

19X7		£
Jan 2	Bank	24

Light and Heat

19X7		£
Jan 14	Bank	18

Advertising and Postage account

19X7		£	19X7		£
Jan 14	Bank	39	Jan 31	Bal. c/d	44
" 23	Cash	5			
		44			44
19X7					
Feb 1	Bal. b/d	44			

T. Albert Capital account

			19X7		£
			Jan 1	Bank	15,000

Drawings account

19X7		£	19X7		£
Jan 17	Bank	50	Jan 31	Bal. c/d	110
" 30	Cash	60			
		110			110
19X7					
Feb 1	Bal. b/d	110			

Wages account

19X7		£	19X7		£
Jan 5	Cash	28	Jan 31	Bal. c/d	140
" 11	Cash	28			
" 19	Cash	28			
" 25	Cash	28			
" 30	Cash	28			
		140			140
19X7					
Feb 1	Bal. b/d	140			

Bilden Const. Co. Ltd

19X7		£	19X7		£
Jan 15	Goods	350	Jan 21	Bank	150
			" 31	Bal. c/d	200
		350			350
Feb 1	Bal. b/d	200			

Sundries and Cleaning account

19X7		£	19X7		£
Jan 22	Cash	13	Jan 31	Bal. c/d	23
" 28	"	10			
		23			23
19X7					
Feb 1	Bal. b/d	23			

Newgate Education Authority

19X7		£
Jan 9	Goods	210

January 31 19X7

	Dr £	Cr £
Cash	435	
Bank	9,424	
Purchases	6,120	
Unac Wholesale Ltd		880
Fixtures and fittings	500	
Evron Fittings Ltd		500
Rent and rates	865	
Insurances	24	
Light and heat	18	
Advertising and postage	44	
Capital account		15,000
Drawings	110	
Wages	140	
Bilden Constr. Co. Ltd	200	
Sundries and cleaning	23	
Newgate Education Authority	210	
Sales account		1,733
	18,113	18,113

Profit and Loss Account for January 19X7

	£	£
Sales		1,733
Less Cost of sales - Purchases	6,120	
Less Closing stock	5,080	1,040
Gross margin		693
Less:		
Wages	140	
Rent and rates	184	
Light and heat	32	
Insurances	2	
Advertising and postage	44	
Sundries and cleaning	23	425
Profit for month		268

Balance Sheet as at 31 January 19X7

		£
Capital introduced 1 January 19X7		15,000
Add Profit for month of January 19X7		268
		15,268
Less drawings for month of January 19X7		110
		15,158

Represented by:

Fixtures and fittings at cost		500
Current Assets		
Stock	5,080	
Debtors	410	
Prepaid expenses	703	
Balance at bank	9,424	
Cash in hand	435	
	16,052	
Less Current liabilities		
Creditors	1,349	14,658
		15,158

Case Problem 2   M. Primel

(1) Points to be made in letter to M. Primel

Information Requirements

   (i)   Total value of goods purchased.

   (ii) Total value of sales.

  (iii) Despite the fact that payment is made in cash, certain expenses may be accruing or, alternatively, been paid in advance and hence invoices and expense records will be needed.

  (iv) A valuation of stock will be needed for any date when profit is to be determined and a balance sheet prepared.

A 'pro forma' profit and loss account with illustrative figures is set out below:

Profit and loss account for the year ended .....

		£
Sales		16,421
Less Cost of sales - Opening stock	2,600	
Purchases	8,950	
	11,550	
Less Closing stock	3,400	8,150
Gross margin		8,271
Less Expenses	2,140	
Depreciation *	600	2,740 *
Net profit		5,531

Such a statement would enable Primel to see how much he could withdraw from the business for his own personal consumption whilst leaving his original capital (in terms of money contribution) intact.

* See (3) below for further explanation.

(2) Points to be raised:
      (i) depreciation as an expense allocation;
     (ii) profit measurement based on concepts of capital maintenance;
    (iii) expected changes in the replacement price of fixed assets.

Primel's fixed assets should be subjected to depreciation and the most appropriate method would appear to be the straight line. This would require a charge against income in each year of:

Sawing equipment $\frac{£5,000}{3}$ = £1,666

Truck $\frac{£4,000}{4}$ = £1,000
                      £2,666

The fact that he has not allowed any provision for this in withdrawing what he regarded as 'profit' is the reason why he foresees difficulty in replacing the assets. (Ignoring any question of changing price levels.)

(3) This question is included to reinforce the student's awareness of the importance of stock in any profit measurement process. It does not appear to be significant in the case of Primel although it is not clear from his comment how he has 'taken account' of it.

(4) The fundamental point which is expected to be made is that the accrual system or accounting attempts to eliminate the differences in figures which exist between transactions and the ultimate cash movement due to the time lag. The accrual concept is an adjunct of the practice of preparing profit and loss accounts for arbitrarily chosen periods.

(5) The limitations of accounting concepts of profit for decision purposes.
      (i) Going concern; this anticipates decisions not yet made.
     (ii) Arbitrary allocation of fixed expenditure.
    (iii) Historic cost data is irrelevant for future action.
     (iv) Data is transaction based and hence excludes intangibles and external
           factors even where these are relevant.
This list is not meant to be exhaustive but to indicate the areas which students at this stage of study could be expected to understand.

Case Problem 3   Mesland Supplies Limited

(1) Accountants are frequently faced with situations where the accounting system
of an organization is less than adequate. This may range from the complete
absence of any systematic recording of transactions to a breakdown of a comprehensive accounting system. The former case tends to be found amongst farmers,
sole traders and small clubs. The latter can occur anywhere and the authors have
encountered it in nationally known companies.

Mesland Supplies Limited, however, is typical of a large number of businesses
where some attempt is made to record direct cash transactions. It is implicit
in these situations that a full double entry system can be completed by using
the cash books and by diligently examining supporting documents such as invoices
and bank statements.

The major practical problems encountered are usually the ascertainment of
debtors and creditors and frequently the inadequate descriptions on cheque book
stubs.

(2) It is recommended that the double-entry system of accounts be adopted using the
following books
   (i) Cash book - bank and cash
   (ii) General ledger for capital, fixed asset and expense accounts
  (iii) Debtors ledger with supporting sales journal
   (iv) Creditors ledger with columns for analysis.

Students would be expected to suggest the usual classification of accounts which
would be found in an enterprise such as Mesland Supplies Limited and to indicate
the basis of entries by referring to the original documents.

(3)

Sales account

19X6	£	19X6	£
Jan 1 Debtors	3,866	Dec 31 Cash	32,838
Dec 31 Profit and loss account	40,140	" 31 "	4,918
		" 31 Bank	2,012
		" 31 Bad debts	42
		" 31 Discount	156
		Debtors	4,040
	40,006		40,006
19X7			
Jan 1 Debtors	4,040		

* Purchases account

19X6	£	19X6	£
Dec 31 Cash	208	Jan 1 Creditors	2,821
" 31 Bank	33,188	Dec 31 Profit and loss account	34,453
" 31 Discount	792		
" 31 Creditors	3,086		
	37,274		37,274
		19X7	
		Jan 1 Creditors	3,086

Wages and Salaries account

19X6	£	19X6	£
Dec 31 Cash	3,048	Dec 31 Profit and loss account	3,048

Motor Expenses account

19X6	£	19X6	£
Jan 1 Prepayment	54	Dec 31 Prepayment	60
Dec 31 Cash	336	" 31 Profit and loss account	450
" 31 Bank	40		
" 31 Bank	80		
	510		510
19X7			
Jan 1 Prepayment	60		

Advertising account

19X6	£	19X6	£
Dec 31 Cash	168	Dec 31 Profit and loss account	848
" 31 Bank	622		
" 31 Amt o/s	58		
	848		848
		19X7	
		Jan 1 Amt o/s	58

Directors' Salaries account

19X6	£	19X6	£
Dec 31 Cash	2,702	Dec 31 Profit and loss account	2,702

Sundry Expenses account

19X6	£	19X6	£
Dec 31 Cash	238	Jan 1 Balance	75
" 31 Bank	892	Dec 31 Profit and loss account	1,137
" 31 Amt o/s	82		
	1,212		1,212
19X7			
Jan 1 Amt o/s	82		

Rent account

19X6	£	19X6	£
Dec 31 Bank	450	Dec 31 Profit and loss account	600
" 31 Amt o/s	150		
	600		600
		19X7	
		Jan 1 Amt o/s	150

Rates account

19X6	£	19X6	£
Dec 31 Bank	720	Dec 31 Bal. b/d	120
		" 31 Prepaid c/d	120
		" 31 Profit and loss account	480
	720		720
19X7			
Jan 1 Prepaid b/d	120		

Fittings account

19X6	£	19X6	£
Jan 1 Bal.	1,000	Dec 31 Depreciation	220
Dec 31 Bank	1,200	" 31 Bal. c/d	1,980
	2,200		2,200
19X7			
Jan 1 Bal. b/d	1,980		

Share Capital account

	£
19X6	
Jan 1 Bal.	10,000

Inventory account

	£		£
19X6		**19X6**	
Jan 1 Bal.	7,254	Dec 31 Profit and loss account	7,254
19X6			
Dec 31 Profit and loss account	9,302		

Retained Earnings account

	£		£
19X6		**19X6**	
Dec 31 Profit and loss account	1,958	Jan 1 Bal.	958
		Dec 31 Bal. c/d	1,000
	1,958		1,958
		19X7	
		Jan 1 Bal. b/d	1,000

Bad Debts account

	£		£
19X6		**19X6**	
Dec 31 Sales	42	Dec 31 Profit and loss account	42

Discount Received account

	£		£
19X6		**19X6**	
Dec 31 Profit and loss account	792	Dec Purchases	792

Discount Allowed account

	£		£
19X6		**19X6**	
Dec 31 Sales	156	Dec 31 Profit and loss account	156

Doubtful Debt Reserve account

	£
19X6	
Dec 31 Profit and loss account	202

Van Disposal account

	£		£
19X6		**19X6**	
Dec 31 Van a/c	800	Dec 31 Bank	600
		" 31 Profit and loss account	200
	800		800

Motor Van account

19X6		£	19X6		£
Dec 31	Bank	800	Dec 31	Van Disposal account	800
" 31	Bank	2,000	" 31	Depreciation	
				Profit and loss account	400
			" 31	Bal. c/d	1,600
		2,800			2,800
19X7					
Jan 1	Bal. b/d	1,600			

Trial Balance as at 31 December 19X6
(4) and (9)

	Trial Balance		Adjustment		Profit and Loss account		Balance Sheet	
	£	£	£	£	£	£	£	£
Sales		36,100		4,040		40,140		
Purchases	31,367		3,086		34,453			
Stock	7,254			9,302	7,254		9,302	
Gross margin c/d					7,735			
					49,442	49,442		
Gross margin b/d						7,735		
Wages and salaries	3,048				3,048			
*Directors' salaries	2,702				2,702			
Advertising	790		58		848			
Motor expenses	510			60	450			
Sundry expenses	1,055		82		1,137			
Rent	450		150		600			
Rates	600			120	480			
Bad debts	42				42			
Discounts	156	792			156	792		
Doubtful debts			202		202			
Van disposal - loss	200				200			
Depreciation -								
Fittings			220					
Van			400		620			
Loss for year c/d						1,958		
					10,485	10,485		
Motor van	2,000			400			1,600	
Fittings	2,200			220			1,980	
Share capital		10,000						10,000
Retained earnings		958			1,958		1,000	
Cash in hand	22						22	
Bank		4,546						4,546
	52,396	52,396						

184

	Adjustment		Balance Sheet	
	£	£	£	£
Stock	9,302		9,302	
Debtors	4,040		4,040	
Repayments:				
Rates	120			
Van insurance	60		180	
Provision for				
doubtful debts		202		202
Creditors - Trade		3,086		
Sundry expenses		82		
Advertising		58		
Rent		150		3,376
			18,124	18,124

(5) The adjustments have been made in (3) and (4) above to illustrate how they would be effected.

(6) The problems associated with the accounting treatment of stock are those of more sophisticated systems than that needed by Mesland Supplies Limited. When a control system is required to keep track of the flow of goods into and out of stores then a choice has to be made as to (a) the valuation process and (b) the assumptions regarding the flow of goods. These latter assumptions are eventually translated into the procedures known as perpetual and periodic inventory, which under the valuation methods of FIFO and AVCO can give rise to different totals for the stock.

Depreciation: Points to be raised:

        (i) Capital maintenance

      (ii) Allocation over time - reasons

    (iii) Methods of allocation

    (iv) Replacement prices

Bad debts are treated in a full accounting system by transferring the amount considered as irrecoverable to a bad debts account and then writing off the total against the gross margin. The timing of the decision to regard the debt as irrecoverable is important as some accountants argue that if the 'sale' and the recognition of the consequent debt occur in the same accounting period then a reduction of sales should take place. However, this practice is rare in the UK. In cases where the debtors recording system is one of memorandum as in Mesland Supplies Ltd, the omission of the bad debt from the Schedule of debtors automatically recognizes the loss. The reason for this is that under such a system the sale is not recognized until the year end adjustment on the sales account.

To bring it to the attention of the users of accounts the position has to be reconstructed by an entry in the accounts of

Dr Bad Debts account ⎫   with total amount regarded
Cr Sales account   ⎭   as irrecoverable

A provision for doubtful debts requires that an amount is set aside to cover the potential loss which may arise due to uncertainty as to the likelihood of the full amount of debts being collected. The amount involved may be established by direct estimation following examination of all debts or by a percentage of all live debts at the end of the accounting period. This latter method would be adopted if sufficient past experience existed to allow some reasonable confidence in the regularity of debts eventually becoming bad expressed as a percentage of all debts.

The entries in the accounting system are:

Dr Profit and loss account   ⎫   with the amount regarded
Cr Provision for doubtful debts   ⎭   as appropriate

This restricts the size of the net profit and thus prevents an over-distribution of the business's funds.

(7) This question is introduced to allow tutors to demonstrate an imprest system for petty cash.

(8) A columnar cash book does provide a record, albeit historic, of the movement of liquid funds through a business. The cash book is capable of being extended to incorporate additional analysis for control purposes such as debtor and creditor total accounts. Such an adaptation is the use of memoranda columns for recording cash discounts given and received. In the case of discounts allowed the net cash received from the debtor is entered into the appropriate debit column in the cash book whilst at the same time in an adjacent memorandum column the amount of discount allowed is entered. The two items are entered as credits (or as one total) in the individual account of the debtor. Eventually the sum of the discounts memorandum column is entered as a debit in the Discounts Allowed account which at that stage completes the double entry.

In the case of Mesland Supplies Ltd, as all entries had been made net of discount then the appropriate accounts had to be adjusted to show the discount effect. (See (3).)

(9) Profit and loss account for the year ended 31 December 19X6

	£	£
Sales		40,140
Less Cost of sales - Opening stock	7,254	
Purchases	34,453	
	41,707	
Less Closing stock	9,302	32,405
Gross margin		7,735
Discounts received		792
		8,527
Less Wages and salaries	3,048	
Directors' salaries	2,702	
Advertising	848	
Motor expenses	450	
Sundry expenses	1,137	
Rent	600	
Rates	480	
Bad debts	42	
Provision for doubtful debts	202	
Discounts allowed	156	
Depreciation - Fittings	220	
Van	400	620
Loss on disposal of van	200	10,485
Loss for year:		1,958
Retained earnings brought forward		958
Loss carried forward:		1,000

Mesland Supplies Ltd
Balance Sheet as at 31 December 19X6

Fixed Assets	£	£	£
Fittings at written down value			1,980
Motor van at written down value			1,600
			3,580
Current Assets			
Stock		9,302	
Debtors	4,040		
Less Provision for doubtful debts	202	3,838	
Prepayments		180	
Cash in hand		22	
		13,342	
Creditors, amounts payable within one year			
Current liabilities	3,376		
Bank overdraft	4,546	7,922	5,420
			9,000
Capital and (reserves)			
Ordinary shares of £1 each			10,000
Loss - (Profit and loss account debit balance)			(1,000)
			9,000

(10) The control of debtors and creditors requires two aspects for consideration. These are:

(i) a supervisory routine to ensure that terms of trade, discounts and references are observed, and

(ii) an accounting system which contains its own independent checking system.

This latter aspect concerns the actual accounting aspect and normally calls for a system of subsidiary books and total accounts which can be constructed independently of the detailed records maintained by those employees engaged on individual accounts of debtors and creditors. Students would be expected to draw up pro forma total accounts with the items which would appear in them.

Note the treatment of debtors and creditors in the case of Mesland Supplies Limited (see (3)) as this is an expedient often adopted by small businesses where the debtor and creditor records are not incorporated into a total accounting system but are worked as a memorandum which only enters the accounting routines as a year end adjustment.

(11) The accounting conventions adopted in the case of Mesland Supplies Limited are (implicitly) the historic cost convention, the accruals convention, the entity convention, the going concern convention, the money measurement convention and the dual aspect convention.

(12) This question has been included to allow students a more extended discussion of matters raised in the text.

(13) The ratio which has most significance in a case such as Mesland Supplies Limited is the Gross Margin Ratio.

Here it is:

$$\frac{7,735}{40,140} \times 100 = 19.3\%$$

This would need to be compared with similar businesses to establish whether it was different from the average expected elsewhere.

Stock turnover appears low at

$$\frac{34,453}{8,278} = 4x$$

It may have been anticipated that with such a business this would have been higher.

Case Problem 4 Thiron Manufacturing Company Limited

(1) Sales Revenue

	£
4 Harpsichords	8,000
2 "	3,000
	11,000

Total expenses

	£	£
Materials	2,000	
	900	
	1,800	4,700
Labour	2,800	
	800	3,600
Overhead expenses	800	
	100	900
Unclassified		400
		9,600
Less work-in-progress		1,800
		7,800

Profit and loss account for year ended 31 December 19X7

		£
Sales		11,000
Less Cost of sales - Expenses	9,600	
Less Work-in-progress	1,800	7,800
Net profit		3,200

(2) The principle of conservatism would be applied in the case of the two harpsichords which Heavenly Music Ltd have agreed to buy. The sale has not been completed by transfer of the goods and so would not be recognized. A specific time has to be decided upon to recognize the event giving rise to a transaction and the actual legal transfer of goods is normally the guide for this.

In relation to the harpsichords sold on a form of hire purchase arrangement, the profit on the sale of the goods is accepted but the interest element is not recognized until payment is made. (Note. Variations on this approach do exist in practice.)

(3) As indicated in (2) conservatism would dictate the treatment of the sales and potential sales in the case of Thiron. Other conventions applied are the historic cost convention as far as costs are concerned and the money measurement concept. Conservatism if applied in all its rigour could result in firms engaged on long term activities not recognizing any profit until the job was complete. This could be a matter of years in some cases. Historic cost accounting can give rise to overstatement of profit during times of rising prices but the debate is lengthy and will not be entered into here. The money measurement concept can exclude from the calculation of profit the opportunity cost of what is probably skilled labour.

(4) Although the organizational form of Thiron Manufacturing Company Limited is that of a limited liability company, the effective position is that it is a form of sole proprietorship for purposes of decision making and rewards. The informal provisions would therefore be most appropriate if they were similar to those of a sole trader. This means that the opportunity cost of his own employment and use of his capital are significant data for him. He could then compare that with the rewards available to him in running Thiron which may be non-monetary as well as monetary.

(5) Cash flow statement - 31 December 19X7

	£	£
Capital supplied		15,000
Sales and debtors	9,000	
Prepayment	900	9,900
		24,900
Outgoings		
Materials	4,700	
* Labour	3,600	
Overhead	900	
Unclassified	400	9,600
Balance as at 31 December 19X7		15,300

* It is assumed that labour payments are made in cash, and are not imputed as Miles Watson's time is.

It can be seen that as a consequence of the year's activity when restricting accounting entries to cash transactions, the net increase is £300. This compares with the accounting conventions profit and loss account which shows that income is £3,200.

(6) Eventually all business transactions will manifest themselves as cash transactions but merely to record cash as evidence of past activity ignores the recognition of both claims of and claims against the business.

A strong case exists for cash flow reporting provided that the future estimates of cash flows are included.

(7) The costs of the product have been arrived at by a matching of outlays with particular units to be sold. A certain measure of allocation is implied by the use of the term overhead. It is not made clear how this was calculated.

This is more usually recognized as a form of job costing when the costs are directly attached to each individual product. The objective of this system is to identify the cost of each product. This is subject to three difficulties: (i) the definition of cost i.e. has a variable or an absorption system been used (implicitly the latter); (ii) the use of conventions means that historic costs, not current are used and (iii) some arbitrary allocation of expenses may well have been used.

(8) In situations where partially finished products are on hand at the end of an accounting period the valuation process is determined by the nature of the physical processes involved. In cases of continuous processes the question of assigning values on an equivalent unit basis applies (see page 247 et seq.). Where there is a job system such as apparently in operation here then the problem is really only one of assembly of the analysed costs. No profit is deemed to have been earned during the manufacturing period so that the cost is one of historic nature only.

(9) All that can be said as far as profitability is concerned is that the margin on sales is $\frac{3,200}{11,000} \times 100 = 29\%$ and that on the basis of the capital introduced the rate of return is $\frac{3,200}{15,000} \times 100 = 21\%$.

(10) Investing the £15,000 at 5% in a risk-free form would yield £750 per annum, but if the £3,200 was achieved consistently on a yearly basis then selecting (say) 12.5% as an appropriate yield then the business would be worth $\frac{£3,200}{0.125} = £25,600$.

(11) Miles Watson could evaluate the business on one of three bases:

     (i)   on the basis of a continuing yield as in (10) above;

    (ii)   on the basis of a safe yield of £750 p.a. with a higher rate of interest applied to the balance of £2,450;

   (iii)   on a net asset value basis (unknown in this case).

Case Problem 5   Inland Tours Limited

(1) Capital required to commence business
     Initial payments   £
     3 Barges   30,000
     Rent   1,000
     Cash margin   1,000
                                       _____
                                       32,000
                                       ======

There would not be any additional long term finance needed to support the working capital as this is self financing provided the forecasts are fulfilled. (See working capital calculations.)

Working Capital Calculations

19X8	April	May	June	July	August	September
	£	£	£	£	£	£
Balance b/f			500	1,020	1,540	2,680
[1] Receipts	600	1,140	1,140	1,140	1,140	1,140
Balance c/f	20					
	620	1,140	1,640	2,160	2,680	3,820
Balance b/f		20				
Licensing etc.	200	200	200	200	200	200
Fuel and mooring	20	20	20	20	20	20
[2] Living expenses	400	400	400	400	400	400
Balance c/f		500	1,020	1,540	2,060	3,200
	620	1,140	1,640	2,160	2,680	3,820

[1] Receipts are based on a 4-week calendar month.
[2] As a limited company is proposed then this item would most probably take the form of director's salary.
[3] Any question of bank interest on the required loan has been ignored.

(2) It is essential when embarking on a new venture or an expansion of an existing enterprise to ensure that the financial obligations incurred are met within the terms of any loan or credit agreements. A cash budget needs to be drawn up to anticipate such requirements. In the case of Inland Tours, it appears that the initial request for a loan of £5,000 may have left the new company somewhat short and may have inhibited the future prospects.

(3) To apply a capital budgeting decision model to Inland Tours Ltd certain assumptions will be necessary in addition to that concerning zero inflation rate.

These are

(1) No first month lag is experienced due to the agency credit arrangement.

(2) All revenues arose on one date.

(3) All expenses arose on one date and that licences and insurances are variable expenses.

(4) That the revenues and expenses all took place on the last day of the year.

(5) That the 10% cost of capital is an annual figure.

Simplifying assumptions such as these are acceptable for ease of calculation in text book examples such as this. In practice the more accurate data would need to be observed.

Inland Tours

Outlay   Present value of annual net cash inflows

$£30,000 - \overline{a_{10|}}^{.1} \times (6,840 - 1,320)$

$30,000 - (6.1446 \times 5,520) = £3,918$

Thus a net present value of £3,918 would suggest that the project is worthwhile.

(4) In considering a loan for a commercial venture, a bank manager will have to examine the prospects for the repayment of both the loan and the interest. Although security may exist in the form of chargeable assets, in this case, the boats, this is not a sufficient reason to lend money. The manager will need to be satisfied that the proposed use of the money will generate sufficient cash to meet the repayments on due dates.

Viewed in this light it can be seen that Inland Tours Ltd could not repay a loan of £5,000 in one year nor, as appears to be the case, a loan of £7,000 in two years.

The forecasts based on one hundred per cent capacity now appear to be critical and a three year span must be subject to doubt.

(5) A review of depreciation methods is called for here. No single method appears to possess such virtues as to eliminate any others so that students may be allowed a reasonable degree of diversity in their answer providing it is supported with a case for the particular method proposed.

(6) This is introduced at this stage to allow tutors to introduce the ideas of external investment by sinking fund methods which have not been described in the text.

Case Problem 6   Lathan Engineering Company Limited

Balance Sheet as at 30 June 19X0

Fixed Assets	Cost £	Depreciation £	Net £
Freehold land and buildings	163,650	18,473	145,177
Plant and machinery	197,000	87,300	109,700
	360,650	105,773	254,877

Investments - Quoted (Market value at 30.6.19X0?)		64,000
Unquoted		151,000

Current Assets		
Inventory	120,160	
Debtors	61,440	
	181,600	

Less:

Creditors: Amounts payable within one year

Trade Creditors	37,650	
Bank overdraft	26,170	
Preference dividend	7,000	
Proposed final ordinary dividend	18,000	
	88,820	92,780

Creditors: Amounts payable after more than one year

Redeemable 19?? [Secured]	(80,000)
	482,657

Share Capital

Ordinary shares of £1 each	180,000
7% Preference shares of £1 each	200,000
	380,000
Share premium account	20,000
General reserve	30,000
Retained earnings	52,657
	482,657

Profit and Loss account for year ended 30 June 19X0

		£	£
Turnover			410,760
Net profit			36,967
Investment income (required for disclosure)	Quoted		3,120
(not required for disclosure)	Other		8,440
			48,527
Preference dividend		14,000	
Ordinary shares dividend			
Interim		9,000	
Proposed final	18,000	27,000	41,000
			7,527
Retained earnings brought forward			45,130
carried forward			52,657

Note. The requirements of this case problem can be varied to restrict the presentation of the final accounts to that compatible with the information supplied in the text. It was felt, however, that tutors would supplement the discussion in the text with the particular requirements of UK company law in so far as disclosure issued were involved. Answers may be supplemented by notes regarding details of interest payments, depreciation etc.

(2) A very general approach is expected to this question and students may respond in a variety of ways. It is useful at this stage to identify specific user Groups and to suggest their possible information needs. The omissions from the accounts may be as important as the information included and in class discussion of this aspect can draw from students ideas as to what may be relevant for the specific user groups.

(3) The gradual extension of accounting disclosure requirements introduced into company law can generally be explained as a response to the need for shareholders and society at large to see that resources entrusted to the directors have been honestly dealt with. Two separate aspects have played their part:

(i) the more sophisticated commercial and financial operations, and
(ii) the acknowledgement that society had legitimate interests in observing the activities of enterprises.

The law has not been used to suggest criteria for the most efficient use of those resources committed to limited companies as it is deemed to be the right of a shareholder to use his own judgement in that regard. The shareholder can, within reason expect that the limited company has used its resources in an honest manner and his course of action regarding the conduct of the business may be to sell his shareholding or attempt to dismiss the directors.

Ratio analysis from the shareholder's point of view may be useful coupled with the market's opinion of a particular share's worth but any further comment on the use of accounting data and its relationship with share prices is best deferred until later studies.

(4) A shareholder will assess the value of his investment on the returns that will come to him from that shareholding. This is in the form of dividends and so the shareholder would most like to have information about the future prospects for dividends. The relationship between earnings and dividends is complex but generally it can be expected that higher earnings figures will lead to higher dividends.

Profit and loss accounts such as that of Lathan Engineering Company Limited are usually supported by summaries of the last five or ten years results in an effort to allow trends to be discerned. Whilst welcome as additional information, caution must be exercised as trends are notoriously complex to use in forecasting.

As a final point the asset base of the company may serve to indicate (i) the level of fresh investment from which profit may be generated and (ii) the extent to which the assets can cover claims against the business.

(5) The accounting tradition of profit measurement has largely been one of matching expenses with revenues. This has tended to emphasize the profit and loss account as the focal point of attention. As a consequence the issues of valuation have been regarded as secondary, and in some quarters, as no concern to the accountant.

Capital maintenance was largely implicit in arguments about what constituted 'capital' expenditure as opposed to 'revenue' expenditure and in the question of the adequacy of depreciation provisions. What was rarely challenged was that transaction based historical cost was the most appropriate form of valuation base.

(6) In the light of (4) above, the information which would most aid a shareholder in evaluating his investment would be forecasts of future results. Some writers have advocated this either as a form of forecast budgets or as cash flow projections. Since more sophisticated analysis of investment involves some estimation of the risk associated with such projections it would be helpful if the standard deviation or variance attached to such activities could be presented. This needs sufficient past experience of similar ventures to satisfy the statistical reliability of such data.

The case for such additional information rests on claims for reduction in uncertainty in the markets and for shareholders to make more formal decisions.

Management usually argues that such information disclosure is harmful to the competitive position of the business; also it is clear that management is reluctant to offer information which, if it proves to be unfulfilled, will be taken as a judgement on their own performance.

(7), (8), (9)   These have been introduced for use at the discretion of tutors.   For wider treatment of these matters students are referred to *Accounting Theory and Practice* by Glautier and Underdown.

Case Problem 7   Olivet Hardware Company Limited

(1)   Statement of Sources and Application of Funds for year ended 31 December 19X8

		£
Sources:		
Arising from operations. Net profit for year		15,500
Add Non-fund items: depreciation		12,100
	loss on disposal of asset	800
		28,400
Disposal of plant		200
Loan from bank		25,000
		53,600
Acquisition of plant		(62,600)
Net outflow of working capital		9,000

Working capital changes

Sources:	Increase in creditors	4,000	
Uses:	Increase in stock	(6,000)	
	Increase in debtors	(6,000)	
Liquidity change		17,000	9,000

Calculation of depreciation

Freehold property 19X8 provision minus 19X7 provision

    £8,000   -£7,500   -   £500

Plant and machinery 19X7.	Cost	Depreciation	
Balance	50,000	30,000	
Less Disposal	8,000	7,000	
	42,000	23,000	
19X8	104,600	34,600	
Difference	62,600	11,600	11,600

Total Depreciation 12,100

∴ Acquisitions = £62,600

(2) Points to be expressed in report
   (i) Stock and debtor expansion
   (ii) Current ratio has gone from 3.4 : 1 to 1.3 : 1 and acid test ratio
        from 1.85 : 1 to 0.6 : 1
   (iii) Increase in profit after interest of £6,000
   (iv) Rate of return on capital employed (ignoring interest)
        19X7, 16%   19X8, 15.5%
   (v) Percentage of assets against which there are external (non-equity)
        claims
        19X7; 10%   19X8; 43%

(3) The loan from the bank introduces an additional element of risk for the ordinary
     shareholder as it will have prior claims against profits to meet interest
     charges and against the assets in the event of inability to meet the interest
     and repayment commitments.

(4) The only ratio available on the basis of given data is the earnings per share
     which is: 19X7; 31.6 p.p.s 19X8; 61.6 p.p.s. If a price/earnings ratio for a
     company engaged in the same industry were known then some guide might be given
     as to the total value of the company.

(5) The increase in net profit has not been matched by an increase in profitability
     as the ratios reveal. However, since this is the first year of the expansion
     there may be future benefits to flow which will correct this. In allowing for
     the increased expenditure for fixed assets it appears to have been overlooked
     that increased activity would require increased working capital. The retained
     profit has now become locked into long term assets and is no longer available
     for payment of dividend. Under circumstances such as these, banks are reluct-
     ant to lend without a condition of non-payment of dividend or by requiring a
     bonus issue of shares to formalize the position.
       The shareholders' interest in the company if expressed as the present value
     of future dividend flows, will require some higher future flow of dividends to
     compensate for the dividends which will now and possibly in the immediate
     future be foregone.

Case Problem 8   Bartle plc

1. To convert the historical cost figures of the profit and loss account, the following are needed:
   - (i)   Cost of sales adjustment;
   - (ii) Depreciation adjustment;
   - (iii) Monetary working capital adjustment and
   - (iv) Gearing adjustment.

   (i) Cost of sales adjustment:

   <u>Note</u>: Although Bartle plc started business on 1 May 19X1, the initial purchase of goods, £400,000, is being treated as 'opening stock')

   Opening stock   £400,000
   Closing stock   £660,000   (six month's purchase)

   Appropriate index for stock
   Opening -   100
   Closing - on assumption of regular increase of index.
       six months purchases during which time the index went
       from 110 to 120
       so average = 115
   Average for the year = 110.

   (a) Restate closing stock at average for year:

   $$£660,000 \times \frac{110}{115} = £631,304$$

   (b) Restate opening stock at average for the year

   $$£400,000 \times \frac{110}{100} = £440,000$$

   (c) Deduct (b) from (a) £631,304 - £440,000 = £191,304

   (d) Compare with movement on HC stock figures

   £660,000 - £400,000 = £260,000
   Cost of sales adjustment, therefore =
       £260,000 - £191,304 = £68,696   (£68,700)

(ii) Depreciation adjustment

$$\text{Depreciation charged} = £200,000$$

to convert to CCA

$$200,000 \times \frac{130}{100} = £260,000$$

$$\underline{\underline{£ 60,000}}$$

Since this is the first year of operation, there is no 'backlog' depreciation.

Check: Asset cost £1,000,000

Convert to CCA

$$£1,000,000 \times \frac{130}{100} = £1,300,000$$

$$\text{1/5th thereof} = £260,000$$

(iii) Monetary working capital adjustment

First calculate net MWC (obviously no opening value)

	30 April 19X2
Trade debtors	£490,000
Trade creditors	£330,000
	£160,000

Movement in year is £160,000 (i.e. 0, to £160,000)

Debtors represents $\dfrac{£490,000}{£1,960,000}$ = 0.25 so that = 3 months sales.

Index therefore is on average $115 + \frac{5}{2}$ = 117.5

i.e. Sales made during February, March and April

midpoint (average) = halfway through March MWCA is calculated

$£160,000 \times \dfrac{100}{117.5}$ = £136,170

MWCA is £160,000 - 136,170 = £23,830

(iv) Gearing adjustment

This adjustment is based on the following formula:

$$\frac{\text{Average borrowings for year}}{\text{Average borrowings plus equity}} \times (\text{COSA} + \text{MWCA} + \text{Add'n'l Dep'n})$$

Equity is taken in this context to be based on CCA balance sheet values and restricted to operating assets.

These are set out below:

	£
CC value of equity	
Fixed Assets (£1,300,000 - 260,000)	1,040,000
Stock £660,000 × $\frac{120}{115}$	688,696
Trade debtors	490,000
	2,218,696
Less Trade creditors	330,000
Net Assets	1,888,696
Financed by: Borrowings (net)	40,000
Equity interest	1,848,696
	1,888,696

So gearing ratio is:

$$\frac{40,000}{1,888,696} \times 100 = 2.1\%$$

Note: Net borrowings:

	£
15% Debenture	400,000
* Taxation	140,000
* Cash	(500,000)
	40,000

* These figures are normally averaged (opening + closing values ÷ 2) but in this case due to only one year's operations, year end values have been used.

The Current Cost Profit and Loss account can now be drafted

Bartle plc. CC Profit and Loss account to 30 April 19X2

	£	£
Historical cost trading profit		580,000
Less Current Cost Adjustments COSA	68,700	
Depreciation	60,000	
MWCA	23,830	152,530
CCA operating profit		427,470
Interest payable	60,000	
Gearing adjustment (£152,530 × 2.1%)	3,203	56,797
CCA profit before taxation		370,673
Taxation		140,000
CCA profit after taxation		230,673
Dividends proposed		120,000
Net CCA profit retained		110,673

Bartle plc. CCA Balance Sheet as at 30 April 19X2

	£	£	£
Fixed Assets			1,040,000
Current Assets			
Stock		688,696	
Debtors		490,000	
Cash at bank		500,000	
		1,678,696	
Creditors: amounts falling due within one year			
Trade	330,000		
Taxation	140,000		
Proposed dividend	120,000	590,000	1,088,696
			2,128,696
Creditors: amounts falling due after more than one year			
15% Debentures			400,000
			1,728,696
Capital and Reserves			
Share capital			1,200,000
Current cost reserve			418,023
Profit and loss account			110,673
			1,728,696

Current Cost Reserve

Revaluation surpluses	£
Fixed assets (1,300,000 - 1,000,000)	300,000
Stock (688,696 - 660,000)	28,696
COSA (Stocks sold)	68,700
MWCA	23,830
	421,226
Gearing adjustment	- 3,203
	418,023

2. The underlying capital maintenance concept of SSAP 16 stems from the original definition of Sir J. Hicks in *Value and Capital* (Oxford U.P., 1946) of profit. Adapted for companies this is:

'A company's profit for the year is the maximum value which a company can distribute during the year, and still expect to be as well off at the end of the year as it was at the beginning'.

The focus is therefore on how 'well off' is calculated and, following the recommendations of the Sandilands Committee, SSAP 16 requires that the operating capacity of the business is the base.

This has been taken generally, but not exclusively, as a form of replacement cost defined as 'value to the business' and revaluations have been made by reference to appropriate index numbers.

3. Where a company has partially financed its net operating assets by borrowing, it is usually the case that these borrowings are set in monetary terms and not subject to the changes affecting the assets. During a period of rising prices, the shareholders benefit at the expense of the lenders to the company and this feature is recognized by the gearing adjustment which allows part of the gains made to be recognized where the CCA would require their transfer to the capital maintenance reserve (Current cost revaluation reserve).

4. Since cash flow accounting is 'current' inasmuch as income and expenditure is at the most recent prices, it can be concluded that a system such as CCA which attempts to make its data 'current' will produce results that are closer to cash flows than historical cost accounting which does not claim to correct the discrepancies between incurred expenditure and its value at consumption.

General Note

The future form of adjustments for inflation is uncertain at the time of writing. SSAP 16 has run its trial period and a proposed successor system ED 35 has virtually been dismissed. In short, ED 35 proposed a simplified version of SSAP 16 with the requirement of a full CCA balance sheet dropped but with CCA profit figures revealed by way of note with 5 years' comparison. It may well be that some form of CPP (Current Purchasing Power) accounting may re-emerge as the champion.

Case Problem 9 The Westbourne Company Limited

	£	£
(1) Sales		12,000,000
Variable costs -		
Manufacturing	4,800,000	
Administrative and selling	2,400,000	7,200,000
Contribution margin		4,800,000
Fixed costs -		
Manufacturing	4,000,000	
Administrative and selling	800,000	4,800,000
Net profit		- 0 -

(2) The chairman's strategy appears to have paid off. There has been a large increase in sales, and the firm is making profits.

(3)	£	£
Sales		15,000,000
Variable costs -		
Manufacturing	6,000,000	
Administrative and selling	3,000,000	9,000,000
Contribution margin		6,000,000
Fixed costs -		
Manufacturing	4,000,000	
Administrative and selling	1,100,000	5,000,000
Net income before taxation and profit-sharing		900,000
Less: Profit sharing pool - 30%		300,000
Net profit before taxation		600,000
Less: Taxation		300,000
Net profit available for distribution		300,000

This statement illustrates the difference between the contribution income approach and the gross margin approach which is used in the case. When the contribution margin approach is employed, net profit before taxation and profit-sharing is £1,000,000 less than the traditional approach. The difference is accounted for by the increased value of closing stock under absorption costing which includes fixed manufacturing overheads (500,000 units × £2 per unit). The chairman's jubilation should be tempered by this fact. The contribution margin approach which is based upon variable costing principles relates profit to sales, which is normally the critical event affecting profitability. It provides therefore, a more realistic approach to the analysis of profitability and profit planning.

(4) Break-even analysis has certain limitations which arise from the assumptions on which it is based, e.g. that fixed costs are constant and that both the variable cost and revenue curves are linear over the relevant volume of output, that volume is the only factor affecting costs, and that both the price of cost factors and of the product produced or sold remains unaffected by changes in the volume of output.

Break-even analysis is useful because it enriches the understanding of the relationship between costs, volume and prices as factors affecting profit thereby enabling management to make assumptions which will assist the decision-making process in the short-run planning period.

(5) The variable costing controversy is related to external reporting and revolves around the question as to whether or not fixed factory overheads should be included in stock. The separation of fixed and variable costs is essential for profit planning as stated in (4) above. The question remains: should not information in a contribution margin form which is useful to management for profit-planning purposes also be available to external users?

(6) Modern theories of management stress the importance of participation. For example, those who argue in favour of participation in budget setting do so on the grounds of greater commitment, motivation and involvement where participation has been introduced. Economic incentives are important. But if economic incentives are to be successful, employees should participate in setting their own objectives which should be consistent with those of the company.

(7)   In recent years industrial democracy - whereby employee representatives are
given a place on company boards - has become a much discussed subject. In the
UK the Report of the Committee of Inquiry on Industrial Democracy (1977)
(Bullock Report) gave opinion on this movement. The report advocated changes in
company law so that an estimated seven million workers would have the right to
elect trade-union based directors on to the boards of companies employing more
than 2,000 people. No action, however, has been taken to implement these
suggestions.

(1) Profit and Loss account for the year ended 31 December 19X7

	Original £	Adjusted Jones Limited £		Adjusted Evans Limited £	
Sales	50,000		50,000		50,000
Cost of sales	30,000	+ 3,000 research & development			
		+ 500 extra depreciation	33,500	- 2,000 off inventory	28,000
	20,000		16,500		22,000
Administrative and selling	10,000	+ 1,000 bad debts	11,000		10,000
	10,000		5,500		12,000
Tax	5,000		2,750		6,000
	5,000		2,750		6,000

(2) Balance Sheet as at 31 December 19X7

	Original		Adjusted Jones Limited			Adjusted Evans Limited		
	£	£		£	£		£	£
Factory at costs		8,000	+ 12,000 revaluation		20,000	+ 2,000 revaluation		10,000
Plant and machinery cost	12,000							
Depreciation	7,000	5,000	500 extra depn.		4,500			5,000
		13,000			24,500			15,000
Inventory	13,000		− 3,000 research & dev.			+ 2,000 slow moving		
Debtors	9,000		− 1,000 provision					
Cash	1,000							
		23,000						
Creditors	11,000	12,000	− 2,250 tax		10,250	+ 1,000 tax		13,000
		25,000			34,750			28,000
Share capital	15,000				15,000			15,000
Retained earnings	10,000		− 2,250 Profit & Loss a/c		7,750	+ 1,000 Profit & Loss a/c		11,000
		25,000	revaluation of factory		12,000	revaluation of factory		2,000
					34,750			28,000
Margin on sales	20%		$\dfrac{5,500}{50,000}$ = 11%			$\dfrac{12,000}{50,000}$ = 24%		
Asset turnover	2		$\dfrac{50,000}{34,750}$ = 1.4			$\dfrac{50,000}{28,000}$ = 1.8		
Return on net assets	40%		$\dfrac{5,500}{34,750}$ = 15.8%			$\dfrac{12,000}{28,000}$ = 43%		

(3) Two companies in a similar situation treat the same items differently. Ratio analysis illustrates that a meaningful comparison of the results of the companies is not possible in this case.

(4) If standardization acts merely as a straight jacket this kind of problem may emerge. However, if standardization necessitates the use of methods of reporting which are consistent with economic reality it will have beneficial effects.

(5) Standardization does not elimiante judgement. The provision for bad debts and depreciation are two examples from this case which necessitate judgement. The treatment of these items should reflect the economic circumstances of a company.

(6) The treatment of research and development expenses is controversial. Where future benefits are expected it can be argued that such expenditure should be deferred to be matched against the future revenue. The US standard requires that all R & D should be expensed, as treated by Evans Ltd. The UK standard distinguishes between research which should be written off and development which may be carried forward and deferred to future periods. (The UK standard is SSAP 13.)

Case Study   Crimicar Components Limited

(1) Bill Leatherbarrow's report should contain the following

	Alternatives			
	1	2	3	4
	£	£	£	£
Unit price	10.00	10.00	9.50	9.00
Sales units	1,000,000	1,050,000	1,100,000	1,200,000
Total	10,000,000	10,500,000	10,450,000	10,800,000
Variable cost	5,000,000	5,755,000	5,225,000	5,184,000
Contribution margin	5,000,000	4,725,000	5,225,000	5,616,000
Fixed costs	3,000,000	3,025,000	3,250,000	3,500,000
Net operating profit	2,000,000	1,700,000	1,975,000	2,116,000
Break-even sales value	6,000,000	6,722,222	6,500,000	6,730,769
Break-even units	600,000	672,222	684,210	747,863
Break-even volume %	60.0	64.0	61.6	62.3

Alternative 4 produces the largest net profit. (However, note that Alternative 1 would produce almost as much profit, but have a lower break-even point.) If the industry sales volume continues to increase as expected, Alternative 4 would put the company in a much better competitive position in the future.

Other factors which management should consider are: (1) the general economic conditions, (2) the firm's access to additional funds and the cost of them, (3) the prices of labour and supplies in the future, (4) the response of competitors to any price decreases, (5) additional working capital which will need to be financed in order to support increased production and sales.

The financial results if the expected increase in sales are only half those predicted:

Unit selling price	£9.50	£9.00
Sales units	1,050,000	1,100,000
Total	9,975,000	9,900,000
Variable costs	4,987,500	4,752,000
Contribution margin	4,987,500	5,148,000
Fixed costs	3,250,000	3,500,000
Net operating profit	£1,737,500	£1,648,000

(2) The risk from the alternatives is a function of the knowledge of the facts surrounding the alternatives and the competence of Crimicar Components Limited. For example, if the company has carried out extremely detailed market research activities, has a high competence in marketing, has adequate resources and dominates the market, the probability of the company making a successful decision is very high. When considering alternatives 3 and 4 full facts need to be known of the company's competitor's competence and their product's cost structure. Given this information each outcome should be assessed probabilistically using a risk profile i.e. the most knowledgeable members of the company can combine this information with their own experience and the company's statistics to guess the likely outcome of each alternative.

(3) If the firm's relationship with its customers is intimate it may go directly to these customers and ask them what they expect to purchase in coming periods. If the firm's relationship with its customers is not close enough to permit it to go to them directly it may obtain the sales forecasts from individual salesmen. A weakness of these approaches is the possible bias of the people making the predictions. Another method is to use the demand and extrapolate from past trends. The most significant factors should be isolated and explicit recognition given to their importance. For example, the future sales of extractor fans is partly a function extractor fans in their kitchens and bathrooms.

(4) Bob Russell's alternative leads to a decrease in net operating profit and a higher break-even point. The firm increases sales which its competitors may otherwise have captured. But the increase in variable costs in achieving this output may pose serious problems for the long run competitive position of the firm.

(5) Capital budgetary implications are associated with alternative 3 (Mayo's modest expansion of plant capacity) and alternative 4 (an extensive modernization programme). D.C.F. calculations should be made for capital investment decisions. These would take account of the firm's cost of capital and additional working capital requirements to support increased production and sales.

(6) Price elasticity of demand is measured by the formula

$$\frac{\text{Proportionate change in quantity purchased}}{\text{Proportionate change in price}}$$

By comparing alternative 1 with alternative 4 in (1) we substitute:

$$\frac{\frac{200,000}{1,000,000}}{\frac{1.00}{10.00}} = 2$$

which indicates that demand for the product is elastic i.e. the increase in sales is greater than the fall in the selling price.

Pricing policy should begin with the question 'What price should we set to earn our desired return on investment?' Therefore demand elasticity is a very important factor affecting this calculation.

Alternative 4 appears to be best from the long run view of the firm. The break-even point is higher than for alternative 1 but the long run position of the firm appears more secure. The higher break-even point is a result of the reduction in selling price. The ratio of variable costs to sales has decreased from 50% for alternative 1 to 48% for alternative 4. Total cost per unit for these two alternatives has decreased from £8.00 to £7.24.